海上联演常识 100 问

邓 波 主编
尹敬湘 副主编

海洋出版社
2020年·北京

图书在版编目（CIP）数据

海上联演常识100问／邓波主编．－－北京：海洋出版社，2020.12（2021.10重印）
（海军工程大学涉外丛书）
ISBN 978-7-5210-0706-0

Ⅰ．①海… Ⅱ．①邓… Ⅲ．①海战-联合演习-问题解答 Ⅳ．①E823-44

中国版本图书馆 CIP 数据核字（2020）第 271213 号

责任编辑：薛菲菲
责任印制：安 淼

海洋出版社出版发行

http://www.oceanpress.com.cn
北京市海淀区大慧寺路 8 号　邮编：100081
中煤（北京）印务有限公司印刷
2020 年 12 月第 1 版　　2021 年 10 月北京第二次印刷
开本：710mm×1000mm　1/16　印张：10.5
字数：156 千字　　定价：68.00 元
发行部：010-62100090　邮购部：010-62100072
总编室：010-62100034　编辑室：010-62100038

海洋版图书印、装错误可随时退换

本书编写组

主　　编　邓　波
副 主 编　尹敬湘
参编人员　姜　俊　程飞霞　吴彦彬
　　　　　段恪忞　聂　忠　金　倩
　　　　　郭　鹏

序

纵横四海，驰骋五洲，是很多热血男儿的梦想与渴望！战风斗浪卫海疆，壮志豪情向深蓝，更是每名海军官兵的抱负与担当！

聚焦人才打赢，矢志亮剑深蓝。68年来，人民海军在建设世界一流海军的逐梦征程上从未停歇。随着"一带一路"倡议的实施和"军事力量走出去"步伐的加快，人民海军坚持践行共同、综合、合作、可持续的安全观，在职能使命、结构编成、作战模式、军事理论、装备技术、人才培养等方面锐意革新，大胆探索，以更加积极开放的姿态参与交流合作，履行大国责任义务，提供国际公共产品。同时，组织和参加海上联演，也逐步成为海军建设的重要课题及军事实践的"新常态"。因为在运筹国际关系、增进战略互信、维护海洋安全、管控海上危机、提升国家形象、展示国威军威、提高作战能力等诸多方面意义重大、影响深远，各类海上联演始终吸引国人眼球，备受官兵关注。例如，新华网评选的2016年国内十大军事新闻就有中国舰艇编队参加"环太平洋-2016"海上联演。当代海军官方微信报道"环太平洋-2016"、中俄"海上联合-2016""科摩多-2016"、中泰"蓝色突击-2016""海上登陆-2016"、东盟防长扩大会海上安全与反恐、中巴海军双边联演等，次次都登上了全国微信公众号巅峰榜十强。

海上联演在网络及新媒体平台的大热，反映了国人和部队官兵对强国强军的热切期盼，也带来了大量亟待厘清的基础性、概念性问题。海军工程大学邓波同志梳理参加"环太平洋-2016"海上联演的收获感受，结合多年的涉外工作实践，编著了《海上联演常识100问》一书，以问答的形式对海上联演进行全面的科普宣传。这是服务实战化教学、服务实战化训练的主动作为和有益尝试，可以说是，创新正当其时，奋斗适得其势。此书填补了国内研究和介绍海上联演的专著空白，适合作为海军院校涉外培训或联演人才集训教材，也可供部队官兵和社会人员阅读参考。

作为一名曾经的海工学子，我认为，此书最令人欣喜的一点就是，编写过程中吸纳了一群对联演及涉外研究充满热情的青年学员。他们思维活跃、勤学好问，所以全书读起来接地气，具有很强的时代感、创新性和吸引力。这从一个特殊的角度，印证了海军事业兴旺发达、后继有人！深蓝的大海是拼搏的故乡，威武的战舰是奋斗的沃土！期待这样的成果更多地出现，共同奏响中国海军的时代强音！

海军新闻发言人 梁阳

于人民海军成立68周年暨首艘国产航母下水之日

目　录

第一篇　海上联演解码

1. 海上联演是怎么回事？ ··· 1
2. 海上联演怎么分类？ ·· 2
3. 海上联演演什么？ ··· 2
4. 海上联演联出了什么？ ··· 2
5. 海上联演的代号有什么考虑？ ································ 3
6. 海上联演的演习规格怎么确定？ ······························ 3
7. 海上联演科目有哪些？ ··· 4
8. 海上联演有哪些阶段？ ··· 4
9. 海上联演要解决哪些关键问题？ ······························ 5
10. 海上联演的基本任务和原则是什么？ ······················ 6
11. 海上联演的主要特点有哪些？ ······························· 6
12. 如何观察判断定位一场海上联演？ ························· 7
13. 海上联演谁来看？ ··· 7
14. 海上联演有哪些主要看点？ ································· 8
15. 海上联演真的必要吗？ ······································· 9
16. 海上联演的目的和意图是什么？ ··························· 9
17. 海上联演有什么作用？ ······································· 10

18. 海上联演会产生怎样的重大影响？ ………………… 10

19. 怎么看待海上联演中的各国关系？ ………………… 11

20. 海上联演中什么最重要？ …………………………… 12

21. 为什么海上联演受到普遍重视？ …………………… 12

22. 海上联演对参演国家和军队间的关系有哪些积极意义？ ……… 13

23. 和平年代需要进行海上联演吗？ …………………… 13

24. 中国举行的规模最大的海上联演是什么？ ………… 14

25. 与中国进行海上联演次数较多、规模较大的国家有哪些？ …… 15

26. 哪个是全球最大规模的海上联演？ ………………… 16

第二篇　海上联演筹划

27. 海上联演方案是什么？ ……………………………… 17

28. 海上联演方案里有什么？ …………………………… 18

29. 海上联演方案怎么定？ ……………………………… 18

30. 海上联演方案的设计目的是什么？ ………………… 18

31. 海上联演方案设计要求有哪些？ …………………… 19

32. 海上联演方案设计需要什么样的专家团队？ ……… 20

33. 海上联演的地点怎么选？ …………………………… 21

34. 海上联演的科目怎么确定？ ………………………… 21

35. 海上联演的作战想定是什么？ ……………………… 22

36. 海上联演的实战背景怎么定？ ……………………… 24

37. 海上联演的"假想敌"怎么设置？ ………………… 24

38. 海上联演备忘录是什么？ …………………………… 24

39. 海上联演筹备计划和实施计划分别是什么？ ……… 25

40. 海上联演文书是什么？ ……………………………… 25

41. 海上联演由谁来定？ ………………………………………… 25

42. 海上联演行动规范有哪些？ …………………………………… 26

43. 海上联演的指挥权怎么分配？ ………………………………… 26

44. 海上联演不同国家怎么统一协调筹划？ ……………………… 27

45. 海上联演前怎么准备？ ………………………………………… 27

46. 除军事项目外，海上联演还包括哪些内容？ ………………… 28

47. 海上联演期间的文体交流活动设置有哪些选择？ …………… 28

48. 海上联演有哪些部位和职能机构？ …………………………… 28

49. 海上联演为什么要设置联合军事专家组？ …………………… 28

50. 海上联演导演组履行什么职责？ ……………………………… 29

51. 海上联演中演习导演的任务有哪些？ ………………………… 29

52. 海上联演考评组是什么？ ……………………………………… 29

53. 海上联演策划组是什么？ ……………………………………… 30

54. 如何确保海上联演的合法性？ ………………………………… 30

55. 海上联演中的法律顾问是什么？ ……………………………… 30

56. 海上联演有哪些方面需要对外沟通磋商？ …………………… 31

57. 海上联演怎样进行对外沟通磋商？ …………………………… 31

58. 怎样做好海上联演对口磋商工作？ …………………………… 32

第三篇　海上联演实施

59. 海上联演怎么训？ ……………………………………………… 34

60. 海上联演怎么联？ ……………………………………………… 35

61. 海上联演怎么保？ ……………………………………………… 36

62. 海上联演胜负怎么定？ ………………………………………… 37

63. 海上联演怎样强化交流合作？ ………………………………… 37

64. 海上联演如何做到统一指挥？ 38
65. 海上联演怎么通信？ 38
66. 海上联演使用的是真枪实弹吗？ 38
67. 只靠计算机模拟能达到海上联演目的吗？ 39
68. 海上联演的安全问题怎么处理？ 39
69. 海上联演怎样防范舰船碰撞？ 40
70. 海上联演中的保密工作怎样做？ 41
71. 海上联演安全怎么管？ 41
72. 如何提高海上联演的实战化水平？ 42
73. 海上联演如何贯穿实战理念？ 42
74. 海上联演复盘检讨是什么？ 43
75. 海上联演中如何判断"伤亡"？ 43
76. 海上联演的效果怎样评估？ 44
77. 海上联演健康问题有哪些？ 44
78. 海上联演的回撤归建是什么？ 46
79. 海上联演总结是什么？ 46
80. 海上联演新闻报道原则是什么？ 48
81. 海上联演新闻怎样报道？ 48
82. 海上联演新闻报道主题有哪些？ 49
83. 海上联演各阶段怎样安排新闻报道？ 50
84. 如何提高海上联演新闻报道的时效性？ 50
85. 海上联演新闻报道怎样塑造军队国际形象？ 52
86. 海上联演新闻报道应该注意哪些方面？ 53
87. 基层官兵在海上联演中如何有效应对媒体？ 53

第四篇　海上联演展望

88. 海上联演的发展趋势是什么？ ················· 55
89. 海上联演怎样解读新装备发展现状与趋势？ ······· 56
90. 海上联演需要在哪些方面重点加强？ ············· 57
91. 海上联演怎么应对未来海上多样化安全威胁？ ····· 57
92. 海上联演人才队伍怎么建？ ····················· 57
93. 院校在海上联演人才培养方面应发挥什么作用？ ··· 58
94. 海上联演新闻报道未来的发展方向有哪些？ ······· 59
95. 海上联演与未来海上作战样式有何相关？ ········· 60
96. 海上联演将来是否会邀请更多国家参加？ ········· 61
97. 如何提升海上联演对海军战斗力建设的贡献度？ ··· 61
98. 新形势将对组织和参与海上联演提出什么新的要求？ ··· 62
99. 新形势下发展海上联演的基本理念是什么？ ······· 63
100. 新形势下海上联演创新发展有哪些着力点？ ······ 64

附　录

附录1　国外重大海上联演概览 ····················· 66
附录2　海上联演常用英语300句 ···················· 73
附录3　海上联演英文缩略语和术语 ················· 104

参考文献 ··· 153
后　记 ··· 155

第一篇
海上联演解码

1. 海上联演是怎么回事？

海上联演，一般是指两个以上军种或不同建制、不同国家军队依据同一想定，在统一导演和组织指挥下进行的海上军事演习。本书是指两个国家或多个国家海军（也可含其他军兵种、海岸警卫队等）共同组织实施或参加的军事演习。海上联演不是单一性的概念，它可以是合同战术战役演习，也可以是单兵种、单军种演习，可以是海上实弹对抗演习，也可以是后勤保障搜救演习。不能把"海上联演"简单地归结为"海军联演"，很多海上联演都是以一种"综合性"演练的形式展开，一场演习往往既包括海上演习部分，也包括陆上及空中演习部分；不论演习是以海上部分为主导，或是海上部分起辅助作用，只要带有海上部分的"综合性"演习，都可以称为海上联演。

2. 海上联演怎么分类？

海上联演，按规模层次，可分为战术海上联演、战役海上联演和战略海上联演；按涉及国家，可分为双边海上联演和多边海上联演；按对象，可分为首脑机关海上联演和实兵海上联演；按形式，可分为实弹海上联演和非实弹海上联演、分段海上联演和综合海上联演；按目的，可分为示范性海上联演、试验研究性海上联演和检验考核性海上联演；按应对威胁的性质，可分为非传统海上联演和传统海上联演。结合国家关系和演练科目，又大致可分为友好国家间以救援、维和、反恐等为主的海上联演，以及同盟国家间以联合作战、协同支援、模拟对抗等为主的海上联演。

3. 海上联演演什么？

海上联演是各国海上参演兵力在近似实战条件和预有想定情况下在海洋或沿海水域进行的作战指挥和行动的综合性演练，也是海军战役战术训练的高级形式。其任务是提高参演国家海军部队的联合作战能力，增进军事交流和沟通合作能力，锤炼各级指挥员组织指挥水平和机关业务技能、出谋划策水平，提高首长、机关部门之间的整体指挥效能；检验海军武器装备编制体制、条令、教材是否符合作战要求，发现问题，总结经验，改进训练和战备工作；研究作战方案和训练方法，探讨新战法，全面锻炼参演部队，提升参演官兵战斗力，为未来联合作战打下基础。

4. 海上联演联出了什么？

海上联演联出了多方面的效益，主要体现在以下三个方面：

一是在国家关系层面，参演军队、海军的交流合作是国家关系的重要组成部分，海上联演在增进各国战略互信、提升战略协作水平、深化战伙伴关系方面发挥了积极作用。

二是在军队关系层面，海上联演拓展了参演军队、海军务实交流合作领域，提升了军队、海军关系水平，增进了参演官兵友谊。

三是在军队建设层面，海上联演科目设置丰富，既有联合防空、海上补给、反潜等常规科目，也包括联合护航、反劫持、搜救等非传统安全科目，参演军队在联合指挥、联合行动、协同保障等方面相互学习借鉴，提高了共同应对新威胁、新挑战的能力，提高了参演官兵的素质和训练水平。

5. 海上联演的代号有什么考虑？

为海上联演命名代号，是世界各国海军的普遍做法，这既能形象地体现海上联演组织者的意图，也符合保密的要求。命名时，首先要给海上联演命一个正义的名称，表明其"正义性"；其次是选择的代号应能对官兵和民众产生鼓舞士气、振奋民心的作用；再次是海上联演代号要能体现出海上联演的性质。海上联演代号通常以时间、地域、任务类别命名，有时也以参演兵力的性质，或是某些政治外交目的来命名，如"和平使命-2017""环太平洋-2016"等。

6. 海上联演的演习规格怎么确定？

一场海上联演规格的高低是由指挥员级别、任务性质、投入兵力以及实战程度等因素决定的。

一是看双方总导演、联合指挥部指挥员和联合指挥机构的人员构成。假如某次海上联演只是一次图上推演，没有实兵实弹，但指挥员级别高，那就是一次高规格海上联演。具体分为以下几种确定方式。

二是看海上联演的任务及性质。海上联演的性质、规划直接决定了联演科目，通常也确定了联演将按怎样的规模进行。如果联演在出访或来访舰艇到来时进行，主要目的是加深了解，增进互信，主要科目为海上通信、编队航行、队形变换，参与舰艇数量较少，联演规格一般也较小；而在一些传统安全或关系到国家政治、经济、领土安全方面的非传统安全领域海上联演中，科目主要包括反潜、防空、登岛、夺岛、反恐、反海盗、搜救等，需要各参与国严密组织，根据具体科目及演习计划部署舰艇和兵力，联演规格一般较大。

三是看参与国的军事实力和地区作用。各国的海军实力不同，在地区事务中的影响力也有大小，如俄罗斯、美国等国主导的海上联演，规模和规格一般较大。

四是看海上联演的实战程度。有的海上联演演练编队反潜、防空等科目，需要参演方具有很高的战略互信。这样的演习往往规格较高，因为参演方军舰上的多种雷达和光电、通信等电子设备都要启动和使用，装备的战术及技术特点要向对方展示。同时参演的舰艇，如果大多是现役主战舰艇，演练实战性较强，兵力较多，那也可以认为是一次高规格的海上联演。

7. 海上联演科目有哪些？

海上联演科目体现参演国的共同关注和需求，也反映出参演国的决心和作战能力。如有的海上联演科目为海上通信、编队航行、队形变换等，这些演练一般在出访或来访舰艇到来时进行，主要目的是加深了解，增加互信。有的海上联演科目为反海盗、反恐、搜救等，这反映了参演方在非传统安全领域的共同关注。有的海上联演科目为编队反潜、防空等，表明参演方具有很高的战略互信。此外，从科目上也可看出海上联演是否具有攻击性，如有的海上联演科目包括登陆、登岛、夺岛等，那无疑是一次进攻性的海上联演。

8. 海上联演有哪些阶段？

海上联演分为演习准备阶段、海上联合行动实施阶段和演习总结阶段。

在海上联演的准备阶段。首先是双(多)边军队进行演习筹划、磋商，制定演习方案。其次是全面展开演习准备，参演兵力进行适应性训练。第三是各方参演分队进行合练、预演。

海上联合行动实施阶段主要围绕联合防空、联合反潜、联合海空寻歼、联合立体夺控岛礁、联合搜救、联合登临检查等科目展开演练。参演各方舰员还可依托舰艇损管模拟训练场开展损管操练，陆战队员可混编开展轻武器实弹射击、直升机滑降、建筑物登攀与滑降、渡海登岛、海岛防御与进攻等联合训练。

在演习总结阶段，双（多）边指挥部组织对联演科目、实施情况、效果评估等进行复盘总结，将联演成果进行成员共享。

9. 海上联演要解决哪些关键问题？

组织海上联演，是提高训练层次、加快转变战斗力生成模式的一个有效办法，也是各国海军训练改革和发展的重要内容。想要组织好一次海上联演，也有一些突出问题需要解决，可概括为以下三个方面。

一是统一认识，解决好"怎么看"的问题。认清开展海上联演是提高信息化条件下联合作战能力的客观要求。在未来战争中，各国海军能否联得上，将直接影响整体作战能力。必须采取海上联演这种方式，使各国海军部队在同一平台上围绕同一课题练指挥、练协同、练战法，提高联合作战能力。

二是立足现实，解决好"怎么联"的问题。关键是要在演习计划上联。对海上联演要实施统一计划、统一指导、统一管理，把海上联演纳入年度军事训练总体规划，进行通盘考虑。承担海上联演任务的舰艇部队要围绕同一课题，做到演训计划方案相互衔接，确保训练计划相吻合、演练方案相匹配。参演各国海军机关和舰艇部队都要成立海上联演组织协调机构，机关要牵头召开联席会议并制订工作计划，形成多方信息互通反馈、相互督促指导、融合保障等机制，确保海上联演按计划实施。同时加大作战指挥和实兵演练对抗力度，努力实现在作战任务上联、在作战指挥上联、在作战协同上联，提高联合作战能力。

三是突出重点，解决好"怎么演"的问题。联合作战是未来战争的基本作战样式，而联合指挥控制又是提高联合作战效率的核心手段。必须紧紧围绕演练课题，突出在指挥体制建立、指挥机构编成、指挥手段运用和指挥重点确定等方面进行演练。

10. 海上联演的基本任务和原则是什么？

海上联演的基本任务是彰显各国维护地区与世界和平与稳定的坚定决心，震慑国内外敌对势力，展示军队、海军形象；学习借鉴外军有益经验，锻炼摔打参演兵力，提高作战能力和强化应对多种安全威胁、完成多样化军事任务的能力。

组织和参加海上联演必须坚持的原则是：战略互惠、对等实施、各方共同准备与实施。

11. 海上联演的主要特点有哪些？

一是目标多元。海上联演往往蕴含着参演各国在政治、经济、军事乃至文化等诸多方面的考虑，通常都把交流互鉴、合作共赢作为海上联演的基本目标。但不同的参演国也有着不同的出发点：有的是为了谋取传统安全利益，体现为军事盟友间的军事合作，意在通过联演提高协同作战能力；有的体现了应对非传统安全威胁的意图，目的在于协力应对国际恐怖主义、自然灾害等非传统安全威胁；还有的是国家之间开展军事交流与合作，力求通过联演加强彼此了解，增进互信。

二是形式多样。海上联演既有单一的战略层次演习，也有战役战术多层次的演习；既有现地实兵演练，也有室内网上作业。有的演习把战略决策、战役指挥和战术行动紧密连接起来，实现从首脑决策到作战平台的无缝连接，多级同步决策、整体联动，既演练战略战役指挥，又演练战术协同配合，使联演既能体现战略思想和战略企图，又能展现战役作战能力和战术技能。

三是军政互动。海上联演是和平时期各国之间增进战略互信、推动务实合作的重要举措。参演各方把军事、政治和外交手段有机结合起来，不仅注重演习的军事成果，而且注重发挥演习的政治效益和外交效益，着力促进军事关系、政治关系的良性互动，可谓"演习搭台，外交唱戏"。

12. 如何观察判断定位一场海上联演？

一是观察演习的企图立案。企图立案是指根据训练科目、目的和训练问题而设想的敌对双方作战企图的方案。通过演习的企图立案，可以了解演习的作战企图和作战背景，读懂参演双方的用意。

二是观察参演的舰艇和装备。例如，如果出动的都是现役主战舰艇，那么其演练实战性较强。如果有登陆舰参加，那就是有登陆、登岛、夺岛等攻击性强的科目。

三是观察演习的具体行动。性能优良的装备需要良好的技术保障水平，更需要参演官兵优良的军事素质和作战素养，这是体现一国海军软实力的重要标志。

四是观察演习规模和持续时间。这在一定程度上可以表明演习的复杂性。

13. 海上联演谁来看？

海上联演可以在各参演国了解情况并同意的情况下安排或邀请观察员国观摩演习。一般可安排或邀请友好国家的国家元首、政府首脑、军队有关领导及演习举办地各级官员等观摩演习。在各参演国知晓并同意的情况下，非参演国可以观摩海上联演。如2016年环太平洋海上联演邀请巴西、孟加拉国、丹麦等观察员国观摩联演；2016年美国与菲律宾间的"肩并肩"海上联演也安排了日本作为观察员国全程观摩。

在组织外国军事观察员观摩海上联演时，通常有以下几点注意事项：

一是充分展示参演国风貌和气度以及军队战斗力。

二是注意了解观察员本国的风俗习惯，避免不必要的误会。

三是时刻注意防间保密问题，防止泄漏军事秘密。

14. 海上联演有哪些主要看点？

看点一：从演习内容看国家间政治关系

军事是政治的延伸，海上联演自然就是当今国际政治的需要和体现。透过海上联演，我们可以观察两国或多国间政治关系的密切程度和发展趋势。一般来说，海上联演是在国家政治、军事、经济关系密切，或者至少是比较密切的情况下进行的。处于政治、军事上严重对立或互为严重安全威胁的国家间，多数不会举行海上联演。如果对立较严重的国家间举行海上联演，那么这就是两国关系出现和解的一个重要迹象，但这种海上联演只可能是没有多少实质内容的象征性联演。非军事联盟国家间举行的海上联演，一般多以非传统安全合作为演习主题，国家间存在加强合作安全的现实需要，演习的公开性较强。

看点二：从演习样式看各国的安全关切

海上联演，按应对威胁的性质分，可分为非传统海上联演和传统海上联演两大类。结合国家关系和演练科目，又大致可区分为友好国家间以救援、维和、反恐等为主的海上联演，以及同盟国家间以联合作战、协同支援、模拟对抗等为主的海上联演。需要说明的是，国际关系的复杂性往往也反映到海上联演的具体样式中。2003年9月，美国、澳大利亚、日本等11国海军在珊瑚海海域举行了代号为"太平洋保卫者"的海上联演，主要科目是海上拦截违禁船只，貌似关切的是非传统安全，实质却是预防大规模杀伤性武器扩散，演习想定及"假想敌"设置都让人嗅到了当年朝核问题波谲云诡的气息。大规模的灾难救援行动，涉及救灾物资和现役、预备役人员动员与远距离投送，以及海陆空多兵种的协调指挥、通信联络和领导层意志的下达，都堪与真正的军事行动相媲美。美泰"金色眼镜蛇"海上联演向来演练的都是传统安全主题，但2005年却将演习重点放在灾难救援上。这是因为2004年12月印度洋海啸灾难发生后，各国都提高了对大地震和大海啸的警惕。进行海上灾难救援联演，既有应对实际威胁的需要，也有军队职能扩展的考虑。

15. 海上联演真的必要吗？

海洋安全形势的恶化、海上恐怖活动的增多、海上自然灾害的频发，都使得加强海上军事合作变得更加必要而紧迫。

首先，军事威慑与军事战略推动海上安全合作大发展。随着和平力量的增长，通过战略威慑遏制战争，延缓战争爆发，制止战争升级，避免或减少战争破坏，日益成为大多数国家的共同选择。国际社会及有关国家开展以海上联演为主要内容的军事合作，可以起到很好的威慑作用，实现地区和世界局势的稳定。

其次，新时期、新形势下缓和紧张局势，建立军事互信机制需要各国加强海上军事合作。"安全困境"的产生在很大程度上是由于各国对对方的军事力量存在认识不清或持错误估计，从而导致双方可能愈演愈烈的军备竞赛。如果各国能在对话、合作的基础上开展广泛的军事交流、互通有无，消除信息不对称，互相观摩海上联演，军备竞赛就可以在一定程度上缓解直至解除。

16. 海上联演的目的和意图是什么？

海上联演可以加强国际海上合作伙伴关系，增强相互协调行动能力，提高参演兵力遂行多种军事行动的能力。纵观世界各海洋大国、濒海国家所举行的双边或多边海上联演，其目的和意图大体可以分为以下三个方面：

一是和平时期提高参演部队战斗力，从演习中学习战争。海上联演最根本的目的之一是在和平时期训练海军部队，保持和提高战斗力，以防止和应对未来潜在的、可能出现的各种海上战争或威胁，同时通过接近实战的训练条件，检验训练成果。

二是对外展示舰艇装备作战技术性能，促进海军技术合作交流。海上联演常常成为装备援售交易的载体，卖方国家可以以此为途径全面展示其武器的性能，买方国家也可以有更多试用和检验的机会。

三是配合国家外交战略。海上联演是对外发送政治信息的一种重要途径，而且在多数情况下，海上联演的政治意义往往超过了其纯粹的军事意义。"军"与"政"的互动程度高低成为判断海上联演成功与否的重要标准。历史上的军事强国屡次通过海上联演达到展示实力、威慑对手、"不战而屈人之兵"的目的。由此看来，海上联演是对外交的有效补充，可以达到其他诸如谈判、斡旋等外交手段无法达到的目的和意图。

17. 海上联演有什么作用？

在当今世界舞台上，海上联演已然成为一种越来越流行的国际军事合作样式。一方面，海上安全局势的复杂化和威胁的跨境化客观上需要加强国际合作；另一方面，世界强国或地区国家集团往往通过海上联演展示其国力、军力，扩大自己的影响力，增强自身的安全系数。

海上联演演练海上联合行动的指挥、协同和保障，可以提高各国海军共同应对海上安全威胁的能力，提高各国参演官兵专业素质，巩固和发展各国伙伴关系，展示各国海军维护地区安全与稳定的决心和能力。

海上联演是和平用兵的积极探索，是军事务实合作的有效形式，也是军事训练的重要手段，可以密切参演军队之间的联系与友谊，加深各国军队间的理解和信任，在深化海军间战略互信、推动军事关系发展，以及促进军队训练水平的提高上发挥积极的作用。

18. 海上联演会产生怎样的重大影响？

海上联演是落实参演国元首共识，增进参演国政治互信，巩固和发展参演国协作伙伴关系，提高参演国协作水平的一项重要举措。同时，军事关系一向是国家间关系的"风向标"，军事关系的发展也将促进参演国政治关系的深化与提升。因此，国家间举行大规模、高水平的海上联演，在深化双方军事合作的同时，也将有助于巩固和提升参演国之间不同等级的战略协作伙伴关系。

19. 怎么看待海上联演中的各国关系？

随着对外军事交往的增加，如今各国海军越来越多地走出国门参与双边或多边海上联演。每次海上联演都有不同的看点，总的来说，演习背景、科目选定、参演装备、战术行动是海上联演最应关注的四个方面，也是充分体现参演国关系的四个方面。

一是从演练编组看，各国参演舰艇一般会进行混编，体现军事互信达到新高度。各方舰艇混合编组将使各国海军官兵更加熟悉彼此武器装备性能以及行动、流程规范，加深相互了解。

二是从演练科目看，各国海军会演练"联合查证识别"等科目。联合查证识别是对疑似敌对目标进行分析确认，共同进行判断。这包括对海上目标和空中目标的识别，即不仅要能够对来自海上的可疑目标查证识别，也要能够对进入或靠近防空识别区的飞机和航空器进行查证识别。

三是从实战效果看，各国海军会组织水面舰艇编队互为条件进行超视距攻防演练，也可能组织潜艇与水面舰艇编队，飞机与水面舰艇、潜艇等进行自主对抗。海上联演联合性、融合性和实战性的增强，必将提高各国海军联合行动、共同应对海上安全威胁的能力。

四是从默契程度看，海上联演不仅是决心和意志的展示，更是默契和能力的体现，特别是不同国家联动式的指挥训练。海上联演任何的作战企图、作战决心和作战计划都不是单方独立确定的，而是通过联席会议进行磋商协调，最终达成共同认可的企图、决心和计划。

五是从安全关切看，多边或双边海上联演，既是履行国际义务，也是保障自身和地区安全的实际需要。如果海上联演有登陆舰艇的参与，有演练岛礁攻防科目，说明参演方在这个问题上有共同的安全关切；如果演练联合保护海上交通线的行动，则有利于维护世界海洋安全与稳定。

20. 海上联演中什么最重要？

表面上看，海上联演的主要目的是训练海军部队，保持和提高海军部队战斗力，防止和应对未来战争威胁，检验海军部队训练成果。从这些角度看，其意义似乎主要在于联演过程。

但实际上，海上联演不仅是军事力量的展示，更重要的是政治层面的较量。因此，其意义更在于联演结果，特别是"军"与"政"的互动情况往往直接左右海上联演的质量与成败。各个历史阶段的海军强国都曾借助海上联演实现过震慑对手、"不战而屈人之兵"的目的。从这个意义上来说，海上联演实际上也是一种外交行为。

21. 为什么海上联演受到普遍重视？

海上联演是在假定情况诱导下进行的海上联合作战指挥和行动的演练，是海上军事训练的高级阶段。随着世界格局的变化和科技的发展，世界军事强国普遍重视海上联演，其原因在于：

一是可以提高参演兵力执行任务的能力。海上联演从实战需要出发，力求在复杂海域、不良天气和复杂多变的情况下昼夜连续实施，尽可能按作战编制安排相关军种、兵种和专业官兵参加，进行协同演练，并注重运用先进手段，以较小的消耗获取最佳效果。如2017年8月，美国、新加坡海军在太平洋海域举行的代号为"太平洋狮鹫-2017"的海上联演，就是旨在增加综合反潜、对地和防空作战能力，加强两军交流互通。

二是可以扩大自身的影响。和平时期的海上联演是军事斗争的一个重要战略工具。一些国家喜欢通过海上联演来增强战斗氛围，提升对对手的威胁力度。例如，2016年10月，在外界盛传朝鲜即将为建党节献礼而进行核试验或发射导弹的情况下，美国、韩国就在朝鲜半岛全海域启动大规模的所谓"不屈意志"海上联演，内容包括反特种部队作战和精准打击陆上设施训练等科目，连"里根"号核动力航空母舰也赶来参加武力示威，释放出强烈的警告信号。

三是可以加强军队间的相互交流。一些海上联演属于双边或多边机制性军事合作交流项目，通过交流指挥和军队演练的经验，提高国家间军队的组织协调能力和共同应对海上威胁的能力，增强安全合作，巩固发展伙伴关系，促进共建安全海洋环境。如2017年11—12月，中国海军与巴基斯坦海军在东海海域举行"朋友-2017"海上联演，双方演练了武器实射、联合搜救、驱离快速小目标等十余项科目，联演战术背景强、实战化程度高。

四是可以进行战争的准备和训练。在敏感海域和潜在危机地区进行海上联演，有利于战争的准备和训练。如2017年7月，由美国海军与乌克兰海军主导，16国参加的"海上微风-2017"联演，虽是例行性演习，但美国升级了参演兵力和参演科目，体现了美国对俄罗斯在黑海方向上施压的战略意图。

22. 海上联演对参演国家和军队间的关系有哪些积极意义？

海上联演是表明国家政治立场，增强双边和多边互信、合作的重要途径。在国际政治上，一个国家不仅需要通过外交途径，公开宣扬政治主张，也需要通过包括军事途径在内的其他方式，显示政治决心与政策取向。

海上联演无论是演习时机，还是科目设置，都是落实参演国元首共识，增进参演国政治互信，巩固和发展参演国友好合作关系，提高参演国协作水平的重要举措。海上联演将会有效加强各参演国军队互信，不断深化务实友好合作，有力维护地区和平与稳定。此外，海上联演也有利于参演各方学习借鉴彼此经验，探索和提高共同应对新挑战、新威胁的能力。

23. 和平年代需要进行海上联演吗？

海上联演是国家、军队之间增进了解互信的一种重要方式，能帮助参演国家的海上力量拓宽战略和战术的眼界，取长补短。举行海上联演还可以提高各国海上力量合作与协同作战的能力，加强情报信息共享，增进相互了解，共同应对海上安全威胁，维护海上共同利益。例如，中国参与的巴基斯坦海军组织的"和平-17"多国海上联演，不仅检验了海军编队护航的水平，同时也增强了打击海上恐怖主义、海上犯罪及进行人道主义救援等非战争军事行动的能力。因此，和平年代仍需要进行海上联演。

24. 中国举行的规模最大的海上联演是什么？

迄今为止，我国举行的规模最大的海上联演是中俄"海上联合-2017"演习。"海上联合"演习是中国、俄罗斯两国海军组织的年度例行性演习，旨在巩固发展中俄全面战略协作伙伴关系。"海上联合-2017"演习分两个阶段组织实施，第一阶段于7月21—28日在波罗的海举行，中国海军合肥舰、运城舰和骆马湖舰远赴俄罗斯波罗的斯克，在波罗的海东南部海域与俄海军波罗的海舰队围绕联合防空、联合登临检查、海上搜救等科目展开了海上联演，是中国海军首次在波罗的海海域与俄海军开展大型海上联演。第二阶段于9月18—25日在日本海彼得大帝湾至鄂霍次克海南部海域举行，中国海军石家庄舰、大庆舰、东平湖舰和长岛船与俄海军太平洋舰队参演舰艇展开了援潜救生、联合反潜、联合防空、联合反舰、联合反恐等科目演习。

演习旨在巩固发展中俄全面战略协作伙伴关系，深化两军友好务实合作，增强中俄两国海军共同应对海上安全威胁、维护地区稳定的能力，进一步提高双方海上联合行动组织指挥水平，研究探索联合遂行各类任务的方法。

演习在总结前五年经验基础上，第一次实现两个阶段同步筹划、高效准备、异地实施；第一次组织了水面舰艇、固定翼反潜巡逻机和舰载直升机协同反潜，中方研发的中俄海上联演专用指挥信息系统首次实现全系统、全要素的部署和检验；第一次完成了援潜救生实艇对接演练，这也是中国海军首次与外国海军共同完成此类高难度、高风险科目。这充分表明中俄海上联演的实战化、信息化、规范化程度得到进一步提升，标志着两国、两军战略互信达到了新高度。

25. 与中国进行海上联演次数较多、规模较大的国家有哪些？

自 2003 年以来，中国海军积极参与联合反恐、海上搜救等非传统安全领域的双边与多边合作，先后与有关国家举行了多次双边和多边联合反恐演习、海上联合搜救演习。这些海上联演，有助于增强参演国家在主权与安全等重大问题上的相互理解和支持；有助于展示中国维护地区安全稳定的坚定决心，震慑分裂势力和恐怖势力；有助于向世界展示中国改革开放和军队现代化建设水平以及军队联合作战能力；有助于拓展中国军事外交的领域和水平，使指挥员开阔视野、增强战略思维能力，使参演部队经受锻炼、提高联合作战能力。

与中国海上联演次数较多、规模较大的国家有巴基斯坦、俄罗斯等。

21 世纪以来，中巴之间举行的主要海上联演有 13 次："海豚 0310"中巴联合海上搜救演习，演练内容为海上搜救、运送伤员、应急灭火、通信、反恐、联合编队等，于 2003 年 10 月 18 日在东海海域进行，中方 3 艘舰艇、巴方 2 艘舰艇参演。"中巴友谊-2005"海上搜救演习，演习内容有联合编队组成、舰艇分区搜救、海上医疗救护等科目，于 2005 年 11 月 24 日在阿拉伯北部海域进行，总共有 4 艘舰艇参演。"和平-07""和平-09""和平-11""和平-13""和平-17"海上多国联演，由巴基斯坦海军于 2007 年发起，每两年举行一次，中国、美国、英国、法国等均参加，演习内容有打击海上快速小目标和编队机动演练、主炮对海射击、联合搜救演练等。中巴亚丁湾反海盗海上联演，演习内容包括两国护航舰艇联合护航、直升机交叉着舰、联合登临、特战队员直升机滑降、直升机空中搜救、模拟航行补给等科目，于 2011 年 4 月在亚丁湾索马里海域进行，共计 4 艘舰艇参演。中巴"喜马拉雅 1 号"，演习内容包括编队会、小艇快速机动、编队运动、航行补给、直升机互降、分航告别仪式等科目，于 2014 年 10 月 1 日在巴基斯坦海域进行，共计 3 艘舰艇和 1 艘潜艇参演。中巴"朋友-2015"，这是中巴海军首次组织的联合反潜、海上对抗等实战化科目演练，内容包括联合护航、临检拿捕和实际使用武器等科目，于 2015 年 12 月 31 日至 2016 年 1 月 1 日在中国东海进行，共有 4 艘舰艇参演。中巴海军海上联演 2016，内容包括编队运动、导弹拦截等科目，于 2016 年 11 月 19 日在卡拉奇海域进行，共有 3 艘舰艇参演。中巴海军海上联演 2017，演习内容有航行补给、编队航行、联合护航和联合防空等科目，于 2017 年 6 月 13 日在卡拉奇海域进行，共有 5 艘舰艇参演。中巴"朋友-2017"联演，演习科目包括武器实射、联合搜救、驱离快速小目标等十余项科目，于 2017 年 11 月 30 日在东海海域进行，共有 2 艘舰艇参演。

中俄之间举行的主要海上联演有 8 次："和平使命-2005"中俄海上联演，在世界反法西斯战争胜利 60 周年，也是苏联卫国战争和中国人民抗日战争胜利 60 周年，于 2005 年 8 月 18—25 日在俄罗斯符拉迪沃斯托克（海参崴）海域及中国山东半岛海域进行，双方均派出军方高级观演团，中方有 60 余艘战舰参演；"和平蓝盾-2009"海上联演，旨在加强两国海军在维护国际公共海域安全稳定方面的交流合作，提高海军在远海与外军联合执行多样化军事任务的能力，于 2009 年 9 月 18 日在亚丁湾西部海域进行，共有 4 艘舰艇参演；中俄"海上联合-2012""海上联合-2013""海上联合-2014""海上联合-2015""海上联合-2016""海上联合-2017"等系列演习是中俄双边框架内规模最大的海上演习，每年举行一次。

26. 哪个是全球最大规模的海上联演？

"环太平洋"海上联演（Rim of the Pacific，RIMPAC）是由美国主导的世界上规模最大的多边海上联演。自 1971 年开始至苏联解体前每年举行一次，苏联解体后每两年进行一次，目的在于保障太平洋沿岸国家海上通道的安全以及联合反恐。"环太平洋-2016"海上联演有 25 国、46 艘水面舰船、5 艘潜艇、200 架飞机以及 25 000 名人员参演。

第二篇
海上联演筹划

27. 海上联演方案是什么？

海上联演方案指的是根据训练科目、目的和训练问题而设想的敌对双方作战企图的方案。通过联演的企图方案可以了解联演的作战企图和作战背景，读懂参演双方的用意。方案一般包括联演想定、联演时间、联演区域、联演科目等细则。

28. 海上联演方案里有什么？

海上联演方案的设计应涵盖联演准备活动、实施活动和总结活动。而在每一项大的活动中又包含着多项具体活动，如联演准备活动通常包括召开准备工作会议、建立导演机构、选择演习场地、编写演习文书、组织演习保障、建立信息保障机制、培训导调和评估人员、首长机关组织指导检查参演兵力的准备工作等主要活动。

这种多层次活动交叉结构的特点，使海上联演形成了一个具有整体性质的大系统。在这个大系统的运转过程中，其内部存在着多种关系需要协调、多种矛盾需要处理、多种问题需要解决，在哪一个环节上考虑不周，都会直接影响海上联演的效果。海上联演方案包含的内容要做到对演习活动进行科学的规划管理、理顺关系、化解矛盾、发现和解决问题，确保海上联演效果。

29. 海上联演方案怎么定？

组织和参加海上联演，制定联演方案是"第一枪"。联演方案的制定要根据联演主导国的外交战略部署及意图，结合其军队、海军发展建设实际需求与外军合作意向，综合考虑国际安全格局、地缘安全态势、地区安全形势、国家关系等因素来统筹论证决策。一般是提前一年以上筹划海上联演的对象国、时间、地点、科目、规模等。向外方通报后，将各方初步协调结果交由相关职能部门研究，提出初步课题联演方案，再商请参演各方进行多轮工作磋商，一致达成最终的联演方案。

30. 海上联演方案的设计目的是什么？

一是以海上联演方案中确立的联演目的规范联演的方向。联演目的是联演所要达到的预期结果。联演目的一经确定，就将成为联演活动的主要依据,引导和规范着围绕联演所展开的全部活动,规定着联演的基本要求。

二是以海上联演方案的设计保证联演的质量。联演准备中大量繁杂的工作需要有统一的筹划,联演的组织实施需要有坚实的理论支持和可供操作的具体程序,而方案设计就是一项基础性工作。做一个形象的比喻,枝繁叶茂的参天大树是因为它植根于沃土,奔流不息的大江大河是因为有流不尽的源头,联演方案就是联演的"根"和"源",而联演方案的设计者就是"植树人"和"挖井人"。常言道,"根深不怕风吹动""为有源头活水来",就联演而言,一个符合客观实际的、能够高屋建瓴统揽全局的方案就如同是联演组织准备的"根基"和"沃土",如同是联演实施中"永不枯竭的源泉"。

31. 海上联演方案设计要求有哪些?

设计一个切合实际的海上联演方案,对于指导联演的组织与实施,确保联演质量,提升参演官兵信息化条件下的作战能力,具有重要的现实意义。为了设计出高质量的联演方案,方案设计者在具体设计时,通常应遵循以下基本要求:

一是以作战任务为牵引。"仗怎么打,兵就怎么练",是联演的基本要求。这一要求,反映了联演的内在规律,体现了联演的本质要求。联演的最终目的是提高战斗力和赢得作战的胜利。

二是以参演装备为基础。各国海军部队由于使命和自然条件的差异,编制装备和训练情况有一定的区别。在设计联演方案时,设计者要充分考虑各个国家海军的不同情况,使方案与参演部队的编制装备状况基本保持一致,保证联演能客观地反映参演部队的实际训练水平,准确评估参演部队的实际作战能力。

三是体现新的作战理念。联演方案的设计要坚持敢于创新、勇于创新的原则,在合理继承的基础上,针对信息化条件下的作战特点和战术的发展,积极探索新的联演思路和新的联演模式,大胆突破传统的思维方式,运用新的作战理念，灵活采用各种设计技巧，使联演方案的设计充满生机和活力。

四是注重提高联演的效费比。注重联演所产生的实际效益，是联演方案设计者应遵循的重要原则之一。在联演组织和实施过程中，通常需要投入相当数量的武器装备、人力资源和时间资源。设计的联演方案是否能在最短的时间内和最小的物质消耗条件下获取最佳的演练效益，也是评价一次联演的重要指标之一。

32. 海上联演方案设计需要什么样的专家团队？

一是军事专家。海上联演是海军军事训练的高级阶段，海上联演整个阶段的进行都是围绕特定的军事问题进行的。海上联演方案设计，是对海上联演活动的整体筹划和安排，同样也是围绕特定的军事问题进行的，而且随着军事理论、作战理念、战法的发展，相应海上联演理念、组织实施的方法也不断变化。因此，在海上联演方案设计中，需要军事专家对海上联演方案中作战背景、主要作战对象、红蓝双方部队的编制体制、主要战法等内容进行研讨设计，并对研讨结果进行分析。

二是装备专家。未来战争形态、作战样式的改变，使得未来作战对装备效能提出了越来越高的要求，也对武器装备的运用提出了更高的要求。在为未来海上战争服务的海上联演中，参演的武器装备种类和数量也越来越多，而且海上联演还可能担负着检验新装备能力的任务。

三是系统专家。在海上联演方案设计领域专家智慧集成过程中，需要研讨设计的主持人，主要负责控制整个研讨过程，包括研讨过程中流程阶段的划分、各阶段的工作和专家工作分配、各阶段进程的控制、各阶段迭代过程的控制、领域专家有效互动研讨的引导等，及时处理研讨过程中出现的各种问题，保证不同领域专家智慧集成的效果。

四是模型专家。海上联演方案设计强调对内容的分析和检验，而对所研讨内容进行定性定量分析，建立相应的模型是不可缺少的。系统专家、军事专家都很难具备熟练掌握各类模型构建的能力，因此需要在海上联演方案设计的专家团队中加入一类精通建模分析技术的专家,给予专家团队对方案内容的分析和检验以有效的支持。

33. 海上联演的地点怎么选?

海上联演大多在专属经济区或者公海上举行,不像陆上联演通常在本国或他国领土上进行。公海是各国海军可以自由航行的海域。至于专属经济区,沿海各国对其虽有所限制,但只拥有以勘探和开发、养护和管理海床上覆水域和海床及其底土的自然资源为目的的主权权利,对人工岛屿、海洋科学研究和海洋环境保护拥有管辖权;其他国家在该区域内的航行、飞越、铺设海底电缆和管道则不受限制。所以海上联演不存在在他国的"主权管辖"的海域和地域上进行,自由度相对较大。可在其参演国的领海、公海、以及事先征得其他国家同意的他国领海内进行。

根据国际惯例,海上联演区域不应该设在下列区域:繁忙的国际航线上,海峡、运河和通航河口附近,靠近他国战斗训练区的地方,国际控制区域或限制飞行的范围,繁忙的捕鱼区,大陆架和公海上的各种设施附近。海上联演实施战斗训练应主要安排在各国的专属经济区以外,并要严格执行保护海洋环境的各项规则。总体来说,对于常态化演习和外国军舰来访时进行的海上联演,一般会选在主办国附近的海域,尽量避开敏感海域,避免引起冲突。通常选在敏感海域的联演都颇有争议,意在展示武力,威慑对手。

34. 海上联演的科目怎么确定?

一般是按照海上联演目的来确定海上联演的任务,再经过参演国商讨,具体确定海上联演的内容和科目。

一是作为一种外交手段。发展参演各国战略伙伴关系,深化参演各国军队间,特别是海军间的务实合作,一般只涉及一些常规的战术动作,如军舰来访时,主要目的是加深了解,增加互信。主要演练海上通信、编队航行、队形变换、海上补给等。

二是提升参演各国海军之间应对非传统安全威胁和挑战的能力。非传统安全是指除军事、政治和外交冲突以外的其他对主权国家生存与发展构成重大威胁的安全问题，主要包括恐怖主义、海盗、地震、海啸等，这往往需要参演各国海军之间相互协助，共同配合。演练一般会包括运动与通信、主炮和轻武器射击、直升机互降、联合营救被劫持商船、临检拿捕、海上防御、海上补给、护航行动、保证航运安全联合行动和实际使用武器演练等。

三是提升参演各国海军之间应对传统安全威胁和挑战的能力。传统安全是指国家面临的军事威胁及威胁国际安全的军事因素，它是以国家主权的维护为核心，也就是通常所说的国家主权安全，国家应对主权被侵犯的战争和军事要素，涉及政治、军事、外交等领域。针对传统安全威胁的海上联演，一般需要参演各国有一定的战略互信基础。

四是有针对性的进攻性演练。一般都是战略盟国之间进行的演习，出动的一般都是现役主战舰艇，除了应对传统安全威胁的演练科目外，还会包括登陆、夺岛、登岛等攻击性很强的内容和科目。

五是全面提升战略伙伴关系和增强战略互信。一般会包含反潜和防空等科目。因为参演各方军舰上的多种雷达和光电、通信等电子设备都要打开和使用，装备的战术及技术特点要向对方展示，需要很高的战略互信基础。

35. 海上联演的作战想定是什么？

海上联演的作战想定是为海上联演提供基本条件的训练文书。它是根据企图立案、训练目的和受训者水平编写的。其编写质量直接影响海上联演的质量。想定的内容通常包括：基本情况、局部情况、要求执行事项、参考资料和附件等多个部分。基本情况是概括反映参演各方的全局基本情况，局部情况是与演习课题有直接关联的具体情况，这两者是作战想定的主要部分。

按训练范围，可分为综合想定和专业想定；按用途，可分为作业想定、演习想定和考核想定；按想定内容，可分为战役、战术、进攻、防御等想定。

为确保联演顺利进行，并使各参演兵力能够进行有意义的互动，需要制定演习想定。演习框架或想定的细节不会公布，目的是保持一定程度的实战性。演习想定与世界任何具体地区无关，与当前或预感的政治或地缘形势无关。若要加强实战化训练，应注重从演习实战背景的设定着眼，依据可能的作战任务，从战役层面的作战筹划到战术层面的兵力行动，从应对非传统安全的一般科目到应对传统安全的核心科目，通盘考虑、一体设计、连贯组织，使参演兵力把任务中涉及的战术行动程序、方法训熟训实，指挥机构把作战中的指挥、协同与战法、谋略运用研深研透。

例如，"环太平洋-2016"海上联演的背景想定为，夏威夷群岛海域被划分为4个虚拟的沿海群岛国。其中，"格里芬岛"是一个自由民主的共和国，其经济在该地区强大，并和"环太平洋"国家有很深的联系。"猎户座岛"是一个军事独裁国，在沿海国中军事最为强大，其领导人热衷扩张主义。由于"猎户座岛"对"格里芬岛"实施了扣留商船、强夺油产品，甚至击沉船只等敌对行为，该地区的海盗行为正在上升。参演国根据联合国决议，组成多国联合部队出兵制止"猎户座岛"对"格里芬岛"的侵略行为，以恢复航行自由，并将"格里芬岛"的一个恐怖主义组织赶出岛外。这样一个实战化演习背景贯穿全程，既包括战役层次的作战筹划，又包含诸多战术行动的具体计划，确保了战役战术层次的有效衔接；既涵盖防空、反舰、反潜、反水雷等传统威胁的军事行动，也包括反海盗、拦截登临检查、人道主义救援减灾等非传统安全威胁的联合行动，确保了各参演国都能安排适当的训练科目，达到各自的训练目标。

再如，"东盟防长扩大会议海上安全与反恐联合演习-2016"海上阶段演习的想定是：为营救被B国抓捕关押的恐怖分子成员，T3恐怖组织于南海南部海区劫持了由A国向B国航渡的B国商船"AVATAR"号，以此要挟B国释放其成员。"AVATAR"号被劫持后，成功向A国的多国协调中心发出求救信号。收到求救信号后，A国多国协调中心组织海上安全特遣部队前去搜救。海上安全特遣部队找到"AVATAR"号后，对其进行了跟踪监视，待确定B国与恐怖分子的谈判破裂后，与B国的陆上反恐特遣部队联合实施"海上风暴"行动，武力解救被劫持船舶。

36. 海上联演的实战背景怎么定？

首先需要对以往战例进行充分研究，借鉴优秀的经验，再对国际及参演国周边地区形势、周边国家军事实力、国家可能遭受的利益冲突和武力威胁进行综合考虑，结合现代战争可能出现的战况，设计海上联演的实战背景。

37. 海上联演的"假想敌"怎么设置？

这首先取决于海上联演科目：有的海上联演演练反海盗、反恐、搜救等，那"假想敌"就是海盗、恐怖分子和受难人员；有的海上联演演练编队反潜、防空等，那"假想敌"就是敌对势力。其次取决于参演的舰艇和装备：如果出动的都是现役主战舰艇，那么其演练实战性较强，"假想敌"很可能是将来战场上会遇到的所有状况；如果有登陆舰参加，那就是有登陆、登岛、夺岛等攻击性强的科目，"假想敌"就是夺取参演国岛屿、侵犯参演国领土的敌对分子。最后取决于演习规模和持续时间：这时的"假想敌"就是官兵对长时间海上联演作战的烦躁和焦虑。

38. 海上联演备忘录是什么？

海上联演备忘录是指参演各方签署的意在提醒各方此次海上联演目的、科目、内容以及各项参演细则和明令禁止行为的文件。

39. 海上联演筹备计划和实施计划分别是什么？

海上联演计划包括海上联演筹备计划和海上联演实施计划。海上联演筹备计划是组织演习的计划和安排，是演习准备和实施的依据。内容包括演习课题、训练目的、训练问题、演习组织、演习地域、演习的性质和方法、演习开始和持续的时间、演习的阶段划分和时间分配、物资保障等，由各国组织演习的部门负责拟制。

海上联演实施计划则是导演部指导整个演习的内部工作文书，根据首长意图、训练目的、演习方式、训练问题、演习时间等拟制。内容一般为演习课题、演习目的、演习时间、演习地域、参演人员、导演机构、调理程序等，通常以文字结合图表表示，由各国组织演习的部门和参演部队共同拟制。

40. 海上联演文书是什么？

海上联演文书是指组织和实施演习的各种文件、图表、资料等的统称。要求准确、规范、清晰、简明，演习前由各国组织演习的机关或演习导演部负责拟制，必要时汇编装订成册。

41. 海上联演由谁来定？

重大海上联演由参演国国家或军队的高级领导决定，总体计划、方案由其审批。参演国国防部行使与外方签署海上联演有关重大协定的代表权力。规模较小或已经机制化的海上联演也可通过其他有关各方均认可的方式予以确定。

一般来说，海上联演重大问题的筹划、磋商、演习方案、计划拟制，演习任务部署，重要涉外事宜把关及经费申领划拨由各参演国海军（如需要，也可包括其他军种）的参谋部门和外事部门共同负责。按照联演科目设置及兵力规模的不同，再交由各职能部门具体落实。通常国外的战役级海上联演方案设计、组织实施由作战部门负责；战术级海上联演方案设计、组织实施由训练部门负责；后勤保障、医疗救护等科目的海上联演方案设计、组织实施可由后勤卫生部门负责。

42. 海上联演行动规范有哪些？

海上联演经验较丰富的组织方和参演方通常会梳理现有的作战条令、战术教范、训练指导法，吸收历年来演训的成熟做法，借鉴各国海上联演的成功经验，编写一套多国海军战术指南和手册，进一步规范海上兵力行动方式方法。例如，"环太平洋-2016"海上联演依据的是北约《多国海军水面作战联合演习手册》《多国海上战术指南与程序》和《多国海上战术信号与机动手册》等文件。这些文件为北约国家之间、北约与非北约国家之间进行联合训练、演习、作战和保障行动提供了较翔实、标准、操作性强的通信组织规定、兵力行动程序、战术协同动作，以及后勤和装备保障规则。联演期间，各国编队参演项目的指挥协同流程、具体实施方法、信号发送程序等均可参考这些文件，从中找到解答。

43. 海上联演的指挥权怎么分配？

进行海上联演时，参演兵力来自不同的国家。因此，要想顺利完成各项联演内容，统一的指挥是十分重要的。目前，从世界各国主要的海上联演来看，指挥方式一般分为两种：集中式和委托式。

集中式指挥就是大家选举出一个国家来指挥这场海上联演，所有参演兵力由这个国家的指挥部统一调度。当然，要想成为总指挥也没那么容易。它要求演习总指挥部要对各国参演兵力的编制装备、战法特点和训练水平有深入的了解，在这种方式中，往往又会设置演习指挥官、战术指挥官和项目指挥官。

委托式则简单得多,可以将不同项目委托给不同国家兵力组织筹划和指挥。演习前只需各国参演兵力共同商定演习方案、制订详细的演习计划、明确各国参演兵力在演习中的任务、行动时机、行动方式与相互关系。演习中,各国参演兵力独立地分别指挥,按照各自既定的任务分别行动就可以了。

44. 海上联演不同国家怎么统一协调筹划?

海上联演在开展前,要进行各类研讨和演习项目的协调,其中就包含演习各方之间的指挥统一和语言规定,这也对参演官兵的语言提出了较高的要求。而建立顺畅的工作机制,简化指挥作业流程,采用高效方法(如舰长模拟舰艇走位、编队运动)口令协同演习、图上推动、启用互通的信息系统,可以大幅度地提高统一指挥效率。例如,中俄"海上联合-2016"演习,中俄双方共同组成联合导演部、联合指挥部和舰艇编队指挥所,统一导调指挥海空参演兵力行动。当时的海军新闻发言人介绍,"海上联合-2016"演习首次启用中俄海上联合专用指挥信息系统,在各级指挥所和各作战单元、平台上能够实现态势共享、文电收发、指挥命令高效互传,通过这个信息化作战平台,基本实现无声指挥,这标志着在中俄联演中拥有共同的指挥信息化协同平台。中俄联演组织实施规范化,在以往基础上,双方总结形成了一整套演习的规范文书和指挥流程等,通过深化和拓展,进一步优化了联演的组织程序和指挥流程。

45. 海上联演前怎么准备?

参演各国需要做好以下准备工作:商定演习的时间、海域、参演兵力规模;向世界公开宣布演习时间、海域,并做好防护警戒巡逻工作,防止其他无关人员或船只误入演习海域;确定具体的演习科目、语言交流方式;协调战役企图、定下战役决心、拟制作战计划和组织战役协同;联合导演部以及指挥所的组织；部队向预定地域投送；建立联合作战部署；后勤保障方面的相关准备工作；参加演习人员的心理疏导等。

46. 除军事项目外，海上联演还包括哪些内容？

通常还包括研讨交流、战术推演、后勤装备保障、安全保卫、新闻宣传、文体交流、外事联络、通信保密等。

47. 海上联演期间的文体交流活动设置有哪些选择？

海上联演期间，通常会为各国参演官兵安排的文体活动包括：主题文艺演出、篮球、足球、拔河、射击等广受官兵喜爱的友谊比赛等。

例如，中俄"海上联合-2014"演习参演官兵开展了拔河、足球、篮球及乒乓球比赛等。

48. 海上联演有哪些部位和职能机构？

海上联演一般会设置联演指挥部，下设指挥、行管、外事、后勤保障、装备保障等小组，由参演各国派遣代表担任相应的岗位。这些机构前期主要负责拟制演习总体计划，明确任务分工及部署，统一全体参演官兵思想。海上联演开始后则负责统筹指挥联演，确保演习的顺利进行。

49. 海上联演为什么要设置联合军事专家组？

组织和参加海上联演，通常成立联合军事专家组（可兼联合导演部）和联合指导组（或称联合指挥所），具体组织、协调演习的准备与实施工作。

根据海上联演的规模和科目设置，联合军事专家组及各方军事专家组通常以参演各国联合参谋部、军队外事部门和海军有关职能部门人员为主，并选拔参演部队精干人员组成，具体负责与各方磋商演习的重大问题，指导、协调参演部队进行海上联演先期准备。联合指导组通常以参演部队首长机关为主组成,协助联合导演部具体负责参演部队的演习准备、演习实施、安全管理和各项保障等。规模较小的海上联演,组织领导模式和领导机构更简练。

50. 海上联演导演组履行什么职责?

海上联演各方都有自己的总导演,负责整个海上联演任务的指挥和导调任务,可以说是海上联演的"大脑"。在联演开始之前,联演各方总导演会在指挥所进行图上推演,为海上实兵演习做好准备。尤其是规模庞大、科目复杂的联演,对导演组的要求更高,也对联演的最终效果起着决定性作用。

51. 海上联演中演习导演的任务有哪些?

海上联演中组织与指导演习的指挥人员称为演习导演。一般设导演和副导演若干人,主要任务是:演习前制订演习计划,审定演习文书,勘察演习海域,确定想定立案、课题和演习方法,组织导调人员学习,落实演习各项准备工作;演习中组织实施演习方案,掌握演习进度和情况,解决演习中遇到的重大问题;演习后进行总结、讲评,以及各项善后工作。其中,执行导演负责整场演练各项计划科目的制订实施,包括制定演习方案、编写导调文书、拟制实施计划、制定评估方案、培训评估人员。

52. 海上联演考评组是什么?

海上联演考评组由参演各国海军中的专家和军官组成,根据预先设定的演习目标,通过定性和定量两类方法进行裁判。定性分析一般用来对演习红蓝双方的战术思想、战术手段进行宏观评判。而在具体评判某一场对抗的结果时，为了真实地模拟出战场上部队的战斗力和损耗，考评组必须要运用数学计算进行定量分析。若是单纯的海上救援或是反恐演习，则根据具体的情况，以该次海上联演所想要达到的目的、确定的标准来确定是否完成了海上联演。

53. 海上联演策划组是什么？

海上联演策划组是针对海上联演的具体实施而成立的。一般的海上联演应该根据不同的演习目的确定不同的环节应由谁指挥，如何会面，何时开始本次联演，若有突发事件，紧急备案是什么。还要根据上级领导的具体意思将本次联演所要体现的内容充分体现出来，以此展示本国的实力或是学习他国的军事经验。这个组织与实施的过程是由军事指挥部的参谋部门根据相关要求进行相关方案的制定，完成并报上级审批同意之后，再通知相关参加单位到达指定地点，在联演结束之后再对联演全过程做个总结。此外，还应与外事部门保持沟通，提前上报本次具体的活动内容和实施情况，保证能够维护国家形象，必要时处理好突发事件。

54. 如何确保海上联演的合法性？

"合法性"是海上联演得以顺利举行的重要基础，分析海上联演的合法性时，主要应该考虑的是法律依据和法律限度。因为海上联演作为一项军事行动，其本身具有很强的政治敏感性，法律授权非常重要，具体应考虑以下三个方面：一是国际法中海上联演相关规定；二是参演国之间达成关于国际联演的合意；三是参演国国内法关于国际联演的许可。相反，如果未有法律依据而进入他国，将构成国际法上严重的违法行为。

55. 海上联演中的法律顾问是什么？

海上联演一般会建立法律顾问制度，为参演兵力配属必要的军法官或专业法律人士，实施伴随法律保障，特别是联演前，负责对参演的各国海军编队指挥员、舰艇长、普通官兵进行涉外法律和有关国家国情、军情、社情、民情教育，增强参演官兵法制意识和形象意识，熟悉海上联演相关法规的基本内容。

56. 海上联演有哪些方面需要对外沟通磋商？

海上联演对外沟通磋商，主要包括演习级别、演习企图、演习时间、演习目的（如反恐、搜救、登陆等）、演习地点、参演兵力、武器装备、演习科目、实施计划、通信保障、后勤保障等。还要勘察演习有关的场地和设施，确定海上联演的课题。

57. 海上联演怎样进行对外沟通磋商？

海上联演磋商是组织和实施海上联演的重要准备工作，主要由参演各方军事专家组依据各国战略意图、前期签订的有关协议，共同商定演习准备与实施的重要问题。在磋商中，各方应适时签署海上联演期间军队临时处于对方领土（领海、领空）的地位协定，以及相关的通信、保密、卫生检疫、装备器材、核放射物质、人员、记者、观摩团进出境、有关装备器材运输、保存等协定，逐步健全配套法律法规，为海上联演提供法律依据。

海上联演磋商通常采取集中磋商与分组磋商相结合的方式进行。集中磋商主要由各方军事专家组组长共同商定关系海上联演全局的重要问题；分组磋商主要按照各方军事专家组内部职能分工，对口商定各军兵种演习方案、分支计划和专项保障等演习局部问题。海上联演磋商通常有若干次，每次磋商的具体议题、时间和地点等应当根据磋商进展情况商定。每轮磋商结束后，通常应当由各方军事专家组共同签署磋商纪要或备忘录。

组织和参加海上联演磋商之前，应当认真研究，精心筹划，周密做好磋商准备；在磋商期间，要坦诚友好，积极协调，求同存异，对重大问题要坚持原则、讲求策略、进退有度，确保实现既定磋商目标。

通常由演习主导方决定,或参演各方共同磋商海上联演的课题科目、代号、时间、地点、形式、参演兵力、保障和准备工作等重要问题。各方依据磋商达成的共识分别进行海上联演准备。海上联演实施前,通常由各方参演指挥机关组成联合指挥机构,共同参加首长机关演习,联合指挥实兵演习。对于规模较小的海上联演,也可根据实际情况和需要,采取其他形式进行。

58. 怎样做好海上联演对口磋商工作?

对口磋商是海上联演准备的必要环节,也是筹划演练实施的重要步骤。认真研究其特点规律和组织方法,对组织筹划好海上联演,提高联演质量和效益具有十分重要的作用。

首先是精心准备。按照"联合、权威、精干、高效"的原则,成立专门的对口磋商组织机构,负责整个筹划演练有关问题的磋商。根据每轮磋商的内容、层次、规格和进度,确立对口磋商班子的具体组成人员。磋商负责人一般由参演指挥机关的主要领导担任,与外方负责人具有相应的地位;磋商成员选择对应军兵种、专业的专家,在知识专长方面相互补充,以形成整体优势。对口磋商前注意收集四个方面的资料,以了解熟悉参演各方的作战理念、思维方式等情况,在磋商中争取主动。一是参演各方军队、海军的编制体制、作战理论、武器装备的战技性能;二是联演的有关方案、计划;三是磋商各方军官的生活习惯和性格特点;四是有关外事交往和外语知识。磋商场地设计包括六项内容:一是悬挂或摆放各方国旗;二是准备音响、多媒体、各种图表;三是按照对等原则,摆放磋商人员座位牌;四是准备好签署磋商文本所需的物品和场所;五是摆放必要的饮料或茶水;六是设置休息和吸烟的场所。必要时,做好双方合影留念的相关准备工作。

其次是规范流程。①预先协调,明确有关事宜。外方进驻后,应立即指定联络员,建立磋商机制。各方磋商班子先碰头会面,采取非正式磋商的方式,互相认识,概略介绍情况;之后各方指挥机关开始展开工作,共同确定磋商内容，制订磋商工作计划，具体明确磋商时间、地点和步骤等。②单方准备，拟制磋商要点。磋商前，对各方情况都要做充分的调查了解，认真分析利弊，进行充分准备，通常要拟制书面磋商要点，并采取适当形式提前通报对方。根据要求，应准备多个语种的版本，其主要内容包括：要协调的主要问题；希望对方做哪些工作；对方可能会有哪些要求；在哪些方面我方可以让步，等等。磋商要点准备质量的高低，直接决定磋商能否实现理想目标。逐个协商，对口协调分歧。按照磋商计划，各部门分头展开磋商。筹划演练需要磋商的内容很多，应根据联演的课题和内容而定，通常包括：筹划演练的基本程序，有关联演会议的议程和参加人员；联演课题的具体内容，如联演企图、定下决心、组织协调、各军兵种的行动方法等。③集中磋商，形成一致共识。在各方对口业务部门协调达成初步共识的基础上，各方的磋商班子集中进行磋商，重点对各部门协调解决不了的问题进行协调，由各方分别陈述已方意见，各方的主要领导拍板定案，形成共同认可的磋商文本后签署执行。

　　第三是灵活应对。①注重沟通交流，建立和谐磋商气氛。磋商前，加强沟通、增进了解、拉近距离，可大大提升磋商效果。例如，可为外方参演首长、机关排忧解难，开展丰富多彩的双边、多边联谊活动，密切感情，为正式磋商铺平道路。必要的感情沟通是搞好磋商的一个重要方面，只有在和谐的气氛中，双方才能开诚布公、诚挚合作，顺利达成一致意见。尊重各方习俗，避免产生政治分歧。海上联演，应避免跨文化交流产生的歧义，尊重各方的政治、军事体制和习惯做法，按照国际军事交流合作的原则办事，不能"以己度人"。②把握磋商技巧，灵活处理各种情况。磋商的过程，常常是问答的过程，恰到好处的提问与答话，有利于推动磋商的进程。提问时，要注意有效性和明确性，突出重点内容。每次只提一两个问题，简明扼要，便于对方答复。答话时，要注意条理性和分寸性。在先弄清对方问话的意图，稍做考虑后做出恰当回答，对不便于正面回答的问题应绕过去或委婉地加以说明并表示歉意，切不可信口开河。当磋商陷入僵局时，高层领导可以主动出面干预，也可以会见对方高层领导或磋商班子，调解矛盾，创造条件使磋商走出僵局，顺利实现理想目标。

第三篇

海上联演实施

59. 海上联演怎么训？

各方军事专家组通常会根据海上联演磋商进展情况，适时指导、协调参演兵力展开演习准备。重大海上联演一般以各方军事专家组为基础，成立各方演习筹备办公室，统一计划和部署演习准备工作，具体协调和督导参演兵力展开演习准备。参演兵力根据实际需要，建立相应的演习准备领导机构，具体组织本级演习准备工作。对于规模较小的海上联演，原则上由参演兵力根据磋商达成的共识，自行实施准备。

组织和参加海上联演，需要认真进行针对性训练，扎实做好理论准备、技术准备和保障准备等。包括：根据演习课题和预定科目，抓好参演首长机关和部队针对性训练；结合演习特点，着眼应对多种安全威胁，开展作战和训练问题研究；结合联演对象国，适当进行外语培训和外事礼仪、安全保密、法制教育等；依托现有指挥信息系统，构建支撑参演行动的技术保障环境；根据海上联演保障需求，做好海上联演的场地、测绘、气象水文、安全警卫和后勤、装备等保障工作。

60. 海上联演怎么联？

海上联演中参演各方指挥控制力量多、语言沟通障碍大、通信装备制式杂、兵力武器协同难，要在短时间形成合力，准确地完成各种战役战术动作，必须解决好以下怎么联的问题。

(1) 构建精干高效的联合指挥体系，是实现"联"的重要基础

①建立联合指挥机构。要根据海上联演的特点和组织指挥的要求，确定联合指挥机构。一是"决策层"联合，确保联合指挥机构的主要决策人员包括参演各国的作战力量，以形成各参演力量联合的决策集体。二是"智囊层"联合，确保组成联合指挥机构的参演各国参谋人员比例适当，专业互补。三是部门设置联合，确保参演国各军兵种相同或相近的职能部门融合，混编各军兵种人员。②设置网状指挥体制。海上联演参战力量多元、行动样式多样，为确保指挥及时、高效，必须适当压缩指挥层次，建立外形扁平、横向联通、纵横一体的网状指挥体制，使参演各国兵力处在同一个信息流层面上，同时接收任务指令，缩短指挥时间，实现实时行动。③采用高效的指挥方式。采取集中指挥、分散指挥与精确指挥相结合的方式，充分调动和发挥参演各国指挥员的积极性，提高海上联演指挥效率，实现对作战力量高效、准确、及时的指挥控制。

(2) 建立互联互通的通信联络，是实现"联"的基本条件

协同体现在海上联演的方方面面，并贯穿始终。协同能力是评估一次海上联演水平高低的重要指标，这对参演各国海上力量指挥通信装备的兼容性提出了很高的要求。某些结盟国家由于有着长期的军事合作关系，通信装备兼容性一般都比较好，甚至参演各国还配备了相同型号的通信装备，使用同一版本的软件系统。如果在那些短期合作国家间举行海上联演，由

于通信装备多数不具有兼容性，要实现直接的互联互通是非常困难的，因此，联合指挥部必须在充分了解各方通信装备和通信体制的基础上，拟定统一的通信联络方法，并采取有效的技术措施，来解决参演各方通信设备之间的互联互通问题，确保信息资源共享、指令畅通和联演行动上的协同配合。例如，为了达成海上联合行动协同一致，美国和相关国家总结并制定了《海上意外相遇规则》和《演习战术1000》等文件，发给参加联演的各国军队，为彼此协同提供便利。

(3)消除语言沟通障碍，是实现"联"的必要前提

解决海上联演中语言沟通问题，各国一般采取为参演部队配备翻译人员的办法。但是，由于海上联演牵涉面广、层次众多，仅仅依靠翻译进行沟通，势必增加译员需求和增大劳动强度。因此，借助现代科技手段，如利用计算机翻译系统来提高工作效率，就成了现实需求。当然，舰艇旗帜、手势、旗语、灯光通信等是各国海军的通用"语"，如果与一些重要的短语相结合，往往会收到意想不到的效果。1999年，埃及与美国、法国、英国、德国等国在地中海沿岸举行"明星"联演时，详细规定了统一的手势、旗语和灯语，与一些重要的军用短语结合，使参演各方得以进行简单、有效的沟通，通过肢体动作，各方马上就能明白对方想要表达的意思。

61. 海上联演怎么保？

海上联演作战保障包括：任务海区分时段、分地域的气象保障；发布航行警告，组织军地舰船对演习相关海域进行清扫和警戒，确保对演习海域有效管控；制定视频导播方案、布设视频采集点，实现联合导演部、指挥部对海上兵力的即时视讯指挥等。即情报保障、通信保障、航海保障、伪装以及对核武器、化学武器、生物武器的防护。

海上联演的指挥手段、侦察情报、通信、机要、测绘、水文气象、安全保密、军需物资油料、卫生勤务、军交运输、野营装备、武器装备、弹药器材、装备维修、经费等专项保障，由各方相关业务部门按照职责分工负责组织或者协调。

62. 海上联演胜负怎么定？

海上联演中的对抗与平时舰队训练中的对抗差别非常大。在平时的对抗中，我们可以给每一名战士配备特殊的对抗设备，并根据士兵"阵亡"的情况来判断输赢。而海上联演往往会模拟一场大的战役，航母、潜艇、飞机都可能会出现其中，这种情况下很难为每台设备和每个战士配备对抗设备。因此，这就需要我们经常在联演中看到的导演部来判断输赢。

这个部门类似电影中的导演，是整场联演的组织者。一旦联演开始，他们就会马上将各方出兵的多少、武器配备情况以及各方指挥官临场的指挥情况，输入到电脑中进行分析。最终，根据电脑提供的模拟结果来判断对抗各方的胜负。

63. 海上联演怎样强化交流合作？

海上联演可为参演各国交流沟通提供一座友谊桥梁，为各国务实合作搭建一个实践平台。基于这样的理念，在港岸阶段，可安排演习开幕式和记者招待会、演习总结会和闭幕招待会、各参演国海军甲板招待会、舰艇开放日活动、文体比赛等系列多边交流活动；在海上演习阶段，可多次安排各参演国官兵交叉登舰观摩学习、相互配合演练，让各参演国海军官兵进行广泛交流与互动，有效增进彼此间的了解和互信，加深理解和友谊。

实践经验表明，要坚持把组织海上联演作为加强务实合作的平台、深化专业交流的平台、不断学习借鉴的平台，把组织各国官兵交流互动、专业学术论坛、训练技能展示、联合行动协同等作为演习组织筹划的重要方面，尽可能多地安排不同层次、不同内容的交流活动，积极推动与各国海军关系务实发展，以开拓创新的理念深化与各国海军的专业交流与合作，以积极求实的心态全面提升与他国海军联合行动的能力。

64. 海上联演如何做到统一指挥？

一场海上联演级别的高低是由双方总导演、联合战役指挥部指挥员和联合指挥机构的人员构成决定的。指挥中不仅要考察参演兵力和装备数量，还要考察参演的军种和兵种构成，各军兵种之间要做好协同合作。

各国参演兵力在演习不同阶段会接受其他参演国不同程度的指挥。在部队集结、实弹射击演练等阶段，各国参演兵力按照事先协商的路线、次序，在组织国的统一指挥下有序进行；在自由对抗阶段，各国参演兵力在事先分配的红蓝双方中分别组成各自的联合指挥部并接受其指挥。指令的发出和被指挥者是否接受指挥都应按照联演前所协商的演习规则进行。

65. 海上联演怎么通信？

海上联演中各国参演兵力可通过电报、话音以及网络相互沟通。个别情况下可能会提供特种装备帮助各参演方进行通信。例如，北约通用的《演习战术 1000》通过卫星通信保障。同时要各国参演兵力立足现有通信装备，挖潜开源，多途径、多手段改装和升级，提升通信装备系统性能。

海上联演一般采用多类型数据链协同互联方案。该方案主要解决各个平台上不同数据链的互联。数据链互联方案的实现关键在于互联节点功能的设计和实现，因而需要对各类数据链的体制进行深入分析，分析各数据链的协议、信息标准和报文格式。而通信系统的接驳一般是经过参演各方详细商议才确定下来，以确保演习期间信息资源共享，指令畅通。

66. 海上联演使用的是真枪实弹吗？

在海上联演过程中，是否使用真枪实弹，这完全要看演习的内容是什么。如果是一场对抗演练，那么各方大多都使用空爆弹或激光模拟弹，不会造成人员伤亡，而且还能体现出演练的效果。不过，在一些重大的海上联演中，还是会进行实弹射击的。参演各方会对弹着点和攻击一方的进攻路线事先做好规定，进攻一方绝对不会误入或进入危险海域。例如，舰炮攻击和火力覆盖就是这样，在真正的实弹射击区域是没有兵力的。而之所以选择实弹射击，是为了营造实战的氛围和环境，让参演官兵真正体验实战的感觉。

67. 只靠计算机模拟能达到海上联演目的吗？

计算机模拟演习智能化程度高，与实战结合紧密，又可大幅度降低海上联演使用经费，目前已经得到了世界各国的广泛关注与运用。各国海军之间通过开展计算机模拟演习，可在探索高度信息化条件下海空目标跟踪监视和指挥作战流程优化等方面互通有无，提升海上作战能力。事实上，常规演习依靠的是现地实兵、实弹、实装对抗，或是运用沙盘进行兵棋推演。而计算机模拟演习是将所有海战场对抗内容全部数字化、虚拟化，攻防效果可直接由计算机按照导演部预先设置判定显示，具有高度的信息化、网络化和联合一体化的特点。通俗地讲，计算机模拟演习与大家熟知的战争类游戏更加相似，是基于真实海战场条件对指挥工具、作战装备和作战行动等客观实体，利用计算机实现的实战化模拟。近年来，各国海上联演的频率不断提高，规模不断扩大，由传统演习向计算机模拟演习转变是海上军事合作的必然之路。

68. 海上联演的安全问题怎么处理？

要保证海上联演过程中水域的绝对安全，首先要加强相关海域的巡逻、警戒，派相应军舰等在附近海域加强侦察与巡逻，一有突发状况及时上报。岸上警戒部队也应做好监视工作，切不可有半点马虎。另外，雷达一定要全时段开放监控，防范来自空中、水面及水下的危险。即便是休整期间，也要做好执勤工作，尤其是对重点岗位的监控，一定要责任到人。

如遇突发状况，如大型海洋生物或者渔船、海盗船误入，应及时上报，并在第一时间保护参演各方舰艇及人员的安全，尽可能将危险系数降到最低，以减小不必要的损失。如果突发状况影响到舰艇及舰上人员安危，应立即采取必要措施以自保，上报经参演各方讨论后再进行下一步的决策，既不贸然出击，也不能束手待毙。

例如，2014年5月20日开始的中俄"海上联合-2014"演习，为了安全起见，中国军方早在5月16日就公布演习区域的坐标和方位，要求过往船只等不要进入该演习区域。按照国际惯例，一个国家公布军事演习的区域和时间，要求其他国家舰船飞机避让，不仅是为了军事上的保密，也是为了对方航行与飞行的安全，避免引发不必要的事故。

69. 海上联演怎样防范舰船碰撞？

舰船碰撞事故是组织和实施一场大型海上联演需要认真关注和防范的问题，特别是大量舰船航经沿海水域及港口附近，或遇到能见度不良的天气时更容易发生碰撞。一般来说，舰船碰撞事故涉及"人、船、环境、管理"系统中的多种因素，但最主要的还是违反海上避碰规则等人为因素所导致的。据统计，80%的海事事故与人为因素有关，而与人为因素有关的舰船碰撞事故的比率更是高达96%。

导致舰船碰撞事故的人为因素主要有四个方面：一是观察瞭望疏忽；二是舰船速度过快，不能作出恰当的预判，导致无法采取有效的避让行动；三是助航设备使用不正确；四是避让处置失误。据统计，有相当一部分事故是在原本有足够的时间操作、但未采取有效避让措施的情况下造成的。在海上联演中，舰艇分属不同国家，且战术机动多，相互协调困难，更应注意防范舰船碰撞。

因此，要有效防范舰船碰撞，应做到以下几点：

一是保持连续的、不间断的观察状态，采取系统的、全方位的瞭望方法，及早发现来舰，及时核对本舰航向。二是采用适宜的速度航行，尤其在能见度不良的情况下，应降低航速。三是正确使用助航设备。四是加强操船人员的技能培训及避碰知识的学习。

70. 海上联演中的保密工作怎样做？

海上联演尽管是以"开放"的姿态与外国军队进行"联"，但是，保密工作底线思维不可放松。该与外方"联"的内容，应充分展示坦诚与开放；不该让外方知道的军事秘密，应严守保密纪律，做好保密工作。

一是牢固树立保密意识。从国外海上联演失泄密情况来看，大部分都是因为保密意识淡薄、思想松懈、心存侥幸引起的。需要把强化保密意识作为保密工作的首要环节紧抓不放，教育引导参演官兵充分认清保密法规的严肃性、窃密泄密形势严峻性、失泄密后果的严重性，从源头上确保约束行为、不越"红线"。

二是全面细致做好准备工作。建立完善保密工作机制，明确责任划分，形成保密责任体系，全程抓好督导落实。严格规范保密载体资料的保管和使用，携带涉密资料、载体外出必须经过审批。严格涉密场所的保密管控、检查督查。

三是严格落实保密制度。演习中的文印工作应指定地点并由专人负责管理，严格文印登记、签收手续，并确定密级，严格控制知密范围。确保每一份文件"可定位、可核查、可追溯、可收回"。演习过程中对全体人员的手机等电子设备收缴，采用机卡分离的方式进行封存管理。加强安检，严格出入审核，确保军事秘密绝对安全。

71. 海上联演安全怎么管？

一是要合理确定管理层次和功能。海上联演中的管理层次和职能设置必须与作战指挥体系实现一体化融合，管理方式与方法必须适应作战编成与作战进程特点，实施网络化、实时化、战场化管理。安全管理工作必须紧贴实战，把战场生存和战场管理结合起来，让官兵明白演习安全需要全体人员相互协作。

二是要实施科学预测和防范。海上联演应做到全员额、全时域、全阶段管理无死角，必须实施全方位预测，组织拉网式排查，实施规范化管理。制定完善可靠的安全预案并组织演练，及时发现问题，防止意外发生。

三是要着力提高参演官兵自我管控能力。必须把学习教育和安全管理工作贯穿演习全过程，筑牢安全工作基础。针对演习特点和自然气候环境，组织官兵熟悉各种安全规定和安全预案。引导参演官兵把全部精力投入到演习当中，增强演习中的安全防范意识。

72. 如何提高海上联演的实战化水平？

海上联演必须把打仗要求落实到联演中去，树立实战化意识。这就要求必须在联演计划、组织、实施全程始终坚持从严、从实战出发，切实把实战化要求贯穿联演全过程，克服指挥训练"程式化"、战术训练"操场化"、基地训练"营区化"的做法，破除图好看、图彩头、图虚名的功利思想，把一切形式主义赶出演习场，把实战意识变为官兵的自觉行动。

海上联演实战化要紧贴作战任务确定演练课题，结合作战进程设置演练内容，依据不同作战方向、地形特点变换演练场地，模拟实际战场构设演练环境，针对作战对手塑造模拟"蓝军"，紧盯问题不放，组织复盘检讨，使参演人员得到前所未有的锻炼和提高。

73. 海上联演如何贯穿实战理念？

一是以实战需求做好海上联演准备。做好思想发动，激励官兵向实战聚焦、为打赢练兵的斗志，采取有效措施，持续掀起实战化训练热潮。统筹演习内容，将实战内容贯穿于演习全过程。在筹划演习时，以提高快速反应能力为重点，将解除伪装、紧急出动、组织攻击等内容贯穿演习始终。以提高战场生存能力为重点，将机动防御、警戒实施等内容贯穿演习始终；以提高复杂条件机动能力为重点，将长距离、多气候条件、昼夜机动等内容贯穿演习始终；以提高信息化条件下作战能力为重点，将融合指挥、人工智能、目标探测最新技术贯穿演习始终。规范演习标准，预先制定各专业演习操作手册，不断完善和规范演习程序，简化演习步骤，达成最优演习方法。

二是按实战要求组织开展海上联演。围绕打仗的需求开展演习。根据使命任务及战时可能担负的作战行动，组织具有实兵演练经验的人员成立课题导调组，科学设置任务课题，将"机动、开设、指控、防卫、保障"五种能力的演练贯穿作战筹划和实战演练全过程，采取"昼训打基础、夜训促提高"的方法，分步细训，专攻精练，锻炼提高全天候作战能力。着眼现代海战特点，从实战需要出发构设战场环境，把技能、智能穿插起来练，把火力单元与保障分队结合起来训，高强度安排演习计划。选择陌生地域，开展舰艇机动、火力攻击、战术指挥等多科目演习。在组训全程开展对抗演练。探索构建演练对抗分队，分阶段随机设置对抗科目，将敌特袭扰、防空袭、反侦察等战术科目和装备应急抢修等应急情况处置演习贯穿于组训全过程，进一步检验指挥员及号手的实战对抗意识。

三是用实战标准检验海上联演成效。完善联演考核制度，建立健全和固化演习考核机构，全面掌握真实演习水平。在定期考核的基础上，灵活采取专项考、综合考、阶段考、集中考等方式，有效督促演习效果落实。

74. 海上联演复盘检讨是什么？

海上联演复盘检讨是为了引导参演人员对照联演目标和演习实践，查找问题，反思履行职责方面存在的差距，思考如何提高能力、改进工作。主要包括总导演对演习基本情况集中讲评、红蓝军导调组、院校专家组、研究咨询组、红蓝双方指挥员依次点评等环节，通过视频回放、现场点评、实例举证、数据分析等方式查找问题、分析原因、研究对策。

75. 海上联演中如何判断"伤亡"？

在海上联演中，组织联演的导演还肩负着一个重要功能，就是裁定联演双方攻击的效果,即是否有"伤亡"。为了使联演达到接近实战的效果,裁判的方法必须科学合理。现代军事演习中,主要通过定性和定量两类方法进行裁判。定性分析一般用来对红蓝双方的战术、打击手段和打击方式等进行宏观评判。而在具体评判某一场打击的结果时,为了真实地模拟出战场上部队的战斗力和损耗,导演部必须运用数学方法进行定量分析。

76. 海上联演的效果怎样评估?

各国在组织海上联演时,会由参演国指挥机构确立演习的企图立案——根据训练科目、目的和训练问题而设想的红蓝双方作战企图的方案,而企图立案所设立任务的完成度直接关系着海上联演效果的评估。

海上联演不仅是军事力量的展示,更是政治层面的较量,因此,"军"与"政"的互动程度同样成为判断海上联演成功与否的重要标准。2003年年末,中国在不到1个月的时间里先后与印度和巴基斯坦两国举行了以搜救为主题的海上联演。在此期间,印度政府提出了有"印巴和平路线图"之称的"12点和平建议"。巴方原则上接受了大部分建议,并由此开启了新一轮印巴关系的缓和与互动。中方在此前后与印、巴双方进行的海上联演不仅巩固了中巴传统友谊,改善和发展了中印关系,更为重要的是促进了印巴关系的缓和,其成功性毋庸置疑。

77. 海上联演健康问题有哪些?

一般来讲,海上联演航程远、时间长、人员密集、环境复杂多变,参演人员不但要承担繁重的任务,还要接受来自海上各种复杂条件的考验,体能消耗和心理负担都较大。需要重点关注防范下列六种身心疾患,采取积极预防措施,确保身心健康,保持战斗力。

一是注意预防"晕动症"。晕船,是晕动症的一种,也是最为常见的航海疾病之一。为了避免非战斗减员,掌握预防晕动症知识很有必要。在联演远航前,应进行海上适应性训练和平衡功能的训练,如通过滚轮、云梯、秋千等进行抗眩晕训练。远航前要备齐预防晕船的药品。

二是警惕海上"职业病"。长时间航海生活会让肠胃、口腔、皮肤等部位频频出状况，如口腔溃疡、牙龈出血、脱发等，这些都是缺乏维生素所导致的问题。随舰医生称它们为海上"职业病"。参演人员由于饮食保障有限、新鲜蔬菜保质期短，出海一段时间以后蔬菜匮乏，身体中需要的多种维生素得不到有效补充。为有效预防维生素缺乏导致的海上"职业病"，医学专家建议应通过科学安排饮食保证膳食平衡，来解决维生素的需求问题。

三是莫要轻视"皮外伤"。参演舰艇在海上受风浪影响，颠簸摇晃，加上舰艇内部舱室狭小、舷梯陡峭，参演人员劳动强度大、精神紧张，稍有不慎，很容易失去平衡。舰艇上钢铁等坚硬质地结构部位较多，一旦发生碰撞或摔倒，容易发生刀割、挤压、扭伤、烫烧伤等意外伤害，可能造成严重的后果。预防意外伤害，需要养成良好的生活习惯、增强安全防范意识，避免疲劳上岗。

四是千万别得"高温病"。参演人员长时间海上暴晒作业，参加户外运动防护不当，易导致皮肤出现红斑、水肿、水泡和脱皮，出现烧灼感或刺痛。晒伤面积大时还会出现全身症状，如发热、怕冷、头痛、乏力、恶心等。为预防晒伤，建议尽量缩短高温下活动时间，穿戴遮阳衣帽。

五是饮食切忌"过把瘾"。到了不同的海上联演国家与海域，当地美食是一大诱惑。新鲜的，从未见过的海鲜、水果、小吃强烈吸引着每名参演人员。如果不多加注意，任由嘴巴"过把瘾"，吃的时候酣畅淋漓，过了几个小时，有人可能就会出现腹痛、腹泻症状，严重的伴有全身乏力、口干、发热等。造成腹泻的感染性因素非常多，但多数是由细菌引起的。霍乱就是一种由霍乱弧菌所引起的急性腹泻疾病，通过直接污染或通过摄入受污染的水和食物进行传播，所以参演人员临行前应口服霍乱疫苗。

六是小心人员"无名火"。海上联演时，由于活动范围狭小、生活单调、工作任务繁重、舱室噪声大等因素持续性影响，参演人员易产生心理和生理疲劳。再加上手机、互联网等无法使用，参演人员心理环境由原来一个开放的、轻松的状态，变为一个长期持续的相对封闭状态，孤独、压抑、寂寞等负面情绪极易使人员烦躁、易怒、"无名火"增加，甚至出现轻度抑郁。

对于海上联演参演人员的异常心理反应，应进行"零心态"调适。

一是价值取向"零偏差"。少数参演人员面对海上艰苦寂寞的生活、高强度的工作，感到受不了，容易导致心理矛盾加重。对此，可提前搞好教育，结合重大节假日组织升旗、宣誓等集体活动，增强参演人员的自豪感和荣誉感。

二是情感沟通"零距离"。海上联演，参演人员远离大陆和社会，要立足现有条件营造信息环境和情感环境，满足参演人员与外界进行信息和情感交流的强烈需求，视情安排参演人员与亲人通话、视频等，让其感受到亲情的关爱和心灵的慰藉。

三是心理问题"零萌芽"。心理问题有负面感染效应，要早预防、早发现、早治疗。开展群体性活动是有效的预防手段，比如组织娱乐活动和体能训练，结合航经海域讲沿岸国风土人情、奇俗异事等，有助于转移参演人员注意力。对已出现不良心理情绪的参演人员，应及时进行心理干预，引导不良情绪得以可控宣泄。

78. 海上联演的回撤归建是什么？

在一次海上联演结束后，各国参演官兵通常会回撤归建。回撤归建主要是组织参演部队由海上联演地域向各自常驻地机动，返营归建。组织回撤归建要针对各方参演官兵普遍疲劳、容易松懈等实际情况，科学制订计划，严格相关措施，做好各项准备，确保按时离境和回撤行动安全。

79. 海上联演总结是什么？

海上联演总结是对海上联演全过程进行全面、系统的总结和讲评活动。通过全面分析研究，使零星、表面的感性认识上升到系统、本质的理性认识。它的根本目的是使每一位参演人员、导调人员和技术保障人员通过重温演练过程，展开战法讨论，实现实践到理论的升华，并回顾检查导调和系统运行情况，以便从成功中获取经验，从失败中吸取教训，从而将演习所得到的经验教训用于今后的军事训练和未来的战争准备中。

海上联演总结的基本内容通常根据演习课题、训练问题、训练目的、训练方法和训练对象等具体情况来确定。一般包括以下几个方面。

（1）演习的概况

主要简述完成海上联演的基本情况，包括演习的课题、目的、任务、持续时间、演习人员及参演国别、军兵种的组成、准备实施的过程，以及演习指导思想、各国海上力量作战编成、各个训练问题的着眼点等内容，从而对海上联演的主客观条件和有利与不利因素进行分析，起到提纲挈领、一目了然的作用。

（2）演习综合评价

海上联演通常涉及参演人员、导调人员、保障人员三类。其中，参演人员是演习主体，因此应对其进行重点评价。主要应侧重于海上联演过程中参演人员对指挥程序的熟悉情况，指挥活动是否及时到位、具有针对性，各部门间的协调情况，以及对本次演习各种规定的遵守情况等。对导调人员的评价应包括海上联演的组织、导调方式和方法，对演习进程的控制和协调等。对保障人员的评价应侧重于海上联演保障系统的运行及维护情况，是否合理地体现了作战的基本情况以及有关军事规则等。演习评价应围绕演习的基本结论，逐次展开对演习成绩和缺点的概括与剖析。演习的基本结论是对海上联演的基本看法，通过综合比较演习情况与演习目的而得出。在基本结论中通常应采用定性和定量分析相结合的方法表述出演习目的所达到的程度，对演习的成绩和缺点进行具体分析，讲清其表现的方面、性质和产生的原因。无论是肯定成绩还是指出问题，都应结合演习中的各种情况判断、决策、处置加以综合分析提高，从理论和实践的结合上，进一步阐明作战原则及其在演习中的运用，使参演人员能够通过演习总结，深化对演习课题、各个训练问题的理解和掌握，并引发对一些重大的、前沿性的理论问题的思考。

(3) 主要经验和启示

对海上联演进行总结,其根本目的还在于从演习中获得经验和启示。因此,在总结时,必须对演习的经验启示进行分析研究和归纳概括,并把它们升华到理性的高度来认识,以便受训者与施训者在今后的军事训练工作中加以借鉴。无论是经验还是启示,都应分项列出,重要的应冠以标题进行重点说明。

80. 海上联演新闻报道原则是什么?

宣扬参演国军队履行国际义务、维护和平使命的积极努力和突出成就,体现参演国军队间开展务实交流与合作的友好姿态,展现参演国军队过硬的技战术素质和自信开放合作的良好形象,营造对参演国有利的周边环境和舆论氛围。

81. 海上联演新闻怎样报道?

海上联演是一种综合的对外展示,这种展示不仅是军事实力层面的,也包括舆论宣传层面的。从战略的角度看,海上联演新闻报道是联演的一个重要组成部分;从政治的角度看,海上联演新闻报道是有深度、有节奏、与外交呼应的舆论战;从舆论的角度看,海上联演新闻报道是以"我"为主、以军促政、以形寓意的对外宣传活动。报道海上联演需注意以下四种意识:

一是有强烈的主体意识。各国派出精锐力量参加海上联演,是深化国家、军队、海军间关系的实际举措,是展示各国军队现代化建设成果和信息化条件下作战能力的重要舞台,是促进海上防务安全领域深化合作的战略需要,具有重要的政治和军事意义,广泛的国际影响。

二是有积极的策划意识。海上联演的报道时间长、课题多、情况复杂、各方面需求高,要做好报道,离不开策划。一是全程策划。要先厘清报道思路,并形成初步的报道计划。二是全员策划。如此长时间、多领域、多点面的报道,在选题策划上,需要每个采访演习的记者都出主意、想思路。三是全维策划。海上联演的意义、目的,参演部队出国前的训练准备情况,远程兵力投送情况,集结后的训练情况,与友军的交往情况等,都要报道好。只有全方位的策划,才能更好地形成报道规模。

三是有牢固的特色意识。海上联演新闻报道不仅要看热闹,还要看门道。从新闻报道的角度说,不能仅仅停留在阶段性、动态性、表面性的报道层面上,而要沉下去,全面深入地报道参演部队的训练、演习、生活、管理等各方面的情况。深入参演部队采访,注重深度报道,写出具有自信、开放、外松内紧等鲜明海上联演特色的新闻报道。

四是有浓厚的整体意识。搞好海上联演报道,离不开整体意识。各国媒体是一个整体。虽然记者来自不同的媒体,要同台竞技,各显神通,但大家的目标是一致的,那就是宣传报道好海上联演,为国家争光,为军队争光,为各国媒体争光。联演新闻报道本身是一个整体。从宣布参演(主消息),到联演过程(动态报道),再到演习结束(联演综述),整个联演的新闻报道形成了一个整体。

82. 海上联演新闻报道主题有哪些?

一是显示参演国海军之间建立互信、构建海洋命运共同体的积极努力。宣传参演国外交政策和参演国海军之间开展互利合作的积极努力,强调开展海上联演有利于增进彼此互信,推进关系发展。

二是突出海上联演主旨。例如,以维和为主旨的海上联演,就要突出其旨在加强与外军在维和领域的交流与合作,提高执行国际维和任务的能力和水平,共同致力于维护地区和世界的和平与稳定。

三是展现参演国军队良好形象。展现参演国军队开展海上联演的水平,展示参演国军队过硬的军事素质和优良作风,塑造和展现参演国军队合作、开放、自信的良好形象。

83. 海上联演各阶段怎样安排新闻报道？

海上联演一般邀请参演国家媒体、记者现场报道，不邀请非参演国方媒体记者。参照通行做法，记者费用自理，联演承办单位为其提供便利。此外，在联演的不同阶段，也会有不同的安排。

一是海上联演开始前：召开媒体吹风会，介绍此次海上联演的目的、意义，提出采访要求。根据参演各方约定，各方统一时间以国防部或军种新闻发言人名义对外公布。

二是海上联演进行中：组织报道海上联演开幕仪式、理论研讨、共同演习、综合演练和闭幕仪式。不定期举行记者吹风会，介绍海上联演进展情况。组织采访参训官兵，多侧面报道海上联演情况。举行联合记者会，请双方观摩团团长共同接受双方记者采访。

三是海上联演结束后：请有关领导接受媒体专访，总结海上联演成果。

84. 如何提高海上联演新闻报道的时效性？

第一要加强学习，提高对海上联演的把握能力。新闻记者要认真系统地学习和研究海军这一信息化军种的知识，把握信息技术给现代海战带来的变化，把握信息化战场的作战流程，认清信息化战场的本质特征，这样在采访时才能够尽快找准"瞄准点"，选准切入点，完成采访任务。一是拓宽知识面，尽可能多地熟悉军兵种尤其是新的兵种专业知识。现代兵种的增加呈加速趋势，兵种知识和技术的更新越来越快，在不同的作战模块组合中，兵种的作用千变万化，如果缺乏这方面的知识，对战场的把握就永远是片面的、模糊的。二是转变观念、改变视角，学会用信息时代的军事思维方法来认识海上联演。信息技术的广泛运用，使信息化战场日益复杂，使用传统的思维方法已无法准确认识和驾驭这台复杂的巨型机器。信息时代的军事思维方法出现了根本性变化。与之相应，新闻记者的思维也必须以变应变。从本质上讲，信息化战争是系统对抗、体系对决，与之相应的是，新闻记者必须学会用系统的观点分析、研究和反映海上联演。

第二要积极探索，改进采写和组织海上联演新闻的方式。新闻采访是在水中抓活鱼，现在水性变了，鱼性也变了，再用老方法抓鱼很可能最终落个两手空。一是基于宣传效果组织海上联演报道。训练转变中的演习变化多、亮点多，正规的新闻媒体发稿数量难以全面反映海上联演，也难以满足官兵的需要。各部队都有一定的宣传力量，有的在海上联演时还办有自己的小报和电视节目。记者可以帮助或指导参演单位的宣传部门，瞄着海上联演写稿，尽可能多地制作新闻作品。二是改变新闻组织方式。信息化战场的复杂性决定了只靠记者和新闻干事孤军奋战，很难在短时间内完成质量较高的稿件，应调动广大官兵的积极性，发动他们写稿。目前，官兵文化素质越来越高，平时稍加指点，就事写事，应该不成问题，这样的稿件往往与官兵距离最近，最鲜活，也最容易引起官兵共鸣。三是积极采用新的传播方式。目前，海战场局域网建设的速度和带宽的提高速度都很快，完全可以利用其传播新闻。在信息技术一日千里的今天，这方面没有技术上的难题，而且占用的信道不会对作战产生影响，媒体有条件把新闻快速传送到每一个战位，贯穿作战全过程。

第三要转变观念，多写适销对路的海上联演新闻作品。要转变新闻写作观念，放弃"高、大、全"式的指导思想，多写"新、短、快、活、实"的稿件。摒弃新闻"八股气"，多写贴近官兵思想、作战、生活的新闻作品。要坚定不移地把人作为新闻的主体突显出来。人永远是新闻报道的主体，海上联演报道也是这样。现代武器高度智能化、战场变得空前透明，有人把作战问题简单化，认为现代战场就是交战双方武器与技术的对决，这是不正确的。再先进的武器和装备也只是人的能力的延伸，在武器装备有代差的情况下，装备差的一方更要发挥人的主观能动性。在武器装备差别不大、没有代差的情况下，战斗中起决定作用的也还是人这一因素。信息化战场大规模使用计算机，大量的计算、统计、逻辑分析等工作由计算机完成，指挥员可以，并且必须把精力放到谋略研究上来，信息化战场将是奇计叠出、异彩纷呈的战场。信息化战场作战时间短，初战可能就是决战，对单兵而言，冲突的强度高过以往任何战场，这就要求单兵不仅要有熟练的技能，更要有出色的心理素质和应变能力。信息化战场必将涌现出一大批与以往有本质不同的新的典型，他们在演习场上体现出的时代特点正是我们应该关注的焦点。在这方面，海上联演报道要与平时报道严格区别开来。

85. 海上联演新闻报道怎样塑造军队国际形象？

海上联演是军队展示国际形象的重要途径，是对外交流的重要形式，是提高国际话语权的重要平台，是国家软实力的重要组成部分。可以综合运用多种传播手段和方式，提高国际新闻传播能力，充分利用海上联演这个舞台，展现军队和平之师、文明之师、威武之师的风采。

一是采取纪实报道手法，彰显英勇善战的军人本色。"纪实"报道，就是通过叙述、描写、夹叙夹议等方式，让受众身临其境，领悟军队能战善战的英勇本色。例如，海上联演开始前，可以通过对海天景象的描绘和拟声词的运用，将读者带入海上联演情境。海上联演前的世界十分静谧，这就为后续的激战埋下了伏笔，让读者怀着一颗惴惴不安的心等待着狂风暴雨的来临。再比如，可以采用比喻的手法形象地体现出军队武器装备的高水平、高标准以及军队英勇善战的威武本色。海上联演报道通过特写化的表现手法达到视觉化效果，通过全景描绘勾勒出立体式场景。海上联演主要报道各国参演军队的演习情况，也可以穿插报道主办国军队后勤装备物资补给情况，展现强大的后勤补给保障能力。纪实报道较少有直接的形象宣传，而是通过"纪实"的方法让受众自己感受、判断和评价军队形象。

二是树立软传播理念，改变军人的"冷硬"形象。传统军人常常被形容的生性鲁莽、冷硬，这在一定程度上影响了新时期军人的形象。军营对于普通百姓来说，是"军事重地，禁止通行"的地方，严格的管制更是给军人的形象蒙上了一层神秘的面纱。基于这种情况，海上联演要树立软传播理念，通过"润物细无声"的报道方式和报道内容，塑造出和平、文明、威武的军人形象。海上联演报道可以通过适当的感性联想，让受众了解各国军人在一些具体问题上，虽然语言不同，但都"一说就明、一点就透"……这些"同行"间的默契，不正是各国海军不断深化协作、加强互信的缩影？"同行"一词既是指各国军舰多次配合，早已熟悉彼此，也是指各国海军之间的默契。

三是采用立体传播手段，融合运用传统媒体与新媒体。军队形象不仅要在平面媒体上体现出来，让受众通过文字表述发挥联想，更要用图文并茂、动静结合的方法，使受众得到更直观、更具视觉冲击、更通俗易懂的海上联演印象。从"传统渠道"到"新兴平台"，实施媒介合作战略，既充分发挥报纸、广播、电视等传统媒体的功能作用，又善于利用新兴媒体，特别是互联网和微博、微信等传播平台，最大限度、源源不断地向世界传递海上联演的正面信息，使置身世界不同地区的受众都能看到参演军队的形象。

86. 海上联演新闻报道应该注意哪些方面？

海上联演新闻报道是思想性与技术性的统一，策划与落实缺一不可的综合集成式工作，前期与后期必须紧密衔接，只有树立打团体赛的思想才能顺利完成任务。由于海上联演报道涉及国家和军队的形象及荣誉，因此"正面报道"的手法不能不提，即直接阐明国家有关方针政策、为国家利益服务的报道。如在2005年中俄"和平使命-2005"联演期间，俄罗斯国防部长伊万诺夫就表示"俄中军演不意味着两国将进行军事行动"等。

87. 基层官兵在海上联演中如何有效应对媒体？

一是强化媒体形象培养，掌握必要技巧。在多国海上联演中，面对媒体和镜头，受访者直接代表本国军队的形象。因此，参演官兵应当做到泰然自若、谨言慎行、不卑不亢、沉着应对。对可能遇到的问题，提前进行充分预想，熟练掌握政策，做到有备而战。

二是用事实说话，扩大对外影响。用事实说话是参演官兵在与记者交流中遵循的基本原则和有力武器。参演官兵在对外交流中要用事实积极宣传本国的军事方针、国防政策、重大问题上的原则立场，以及在维和、反恐、人道主义救援等方面取得的成就。

三是准确把握对外口径，严守政策和安全底线。海上联演工作政策性、敏感性强，严守政策和安全底线是参演官兵接受采访时的基本要求，必须严格按照对外表态口径和有关政策规定展开，特别是涉及重大、敏感事项要慎之又慎，坚决避免言语不当、授人以柄。严格遵守保密规定，严防把关不严、密从口出。

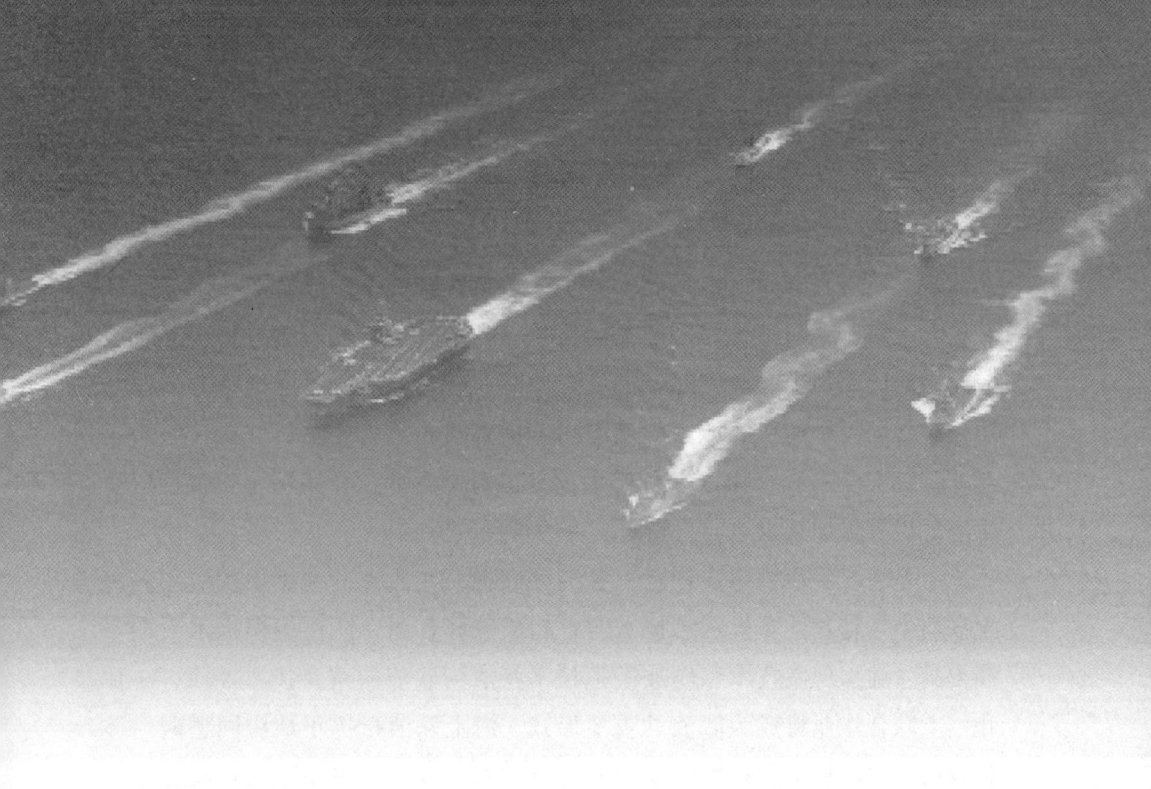

第四篇

海上联演展望

88. 海上联演的发展趋势是什么?

众所周知,海上联演是一种近似实战的综合性演练,是海军军事训练的最高级阶段,其目的既是为了提高部队作战能力,更是为了彰显一个国家的综合国力,并起到军事震慑的作用。如美国与其盟国举行的美日、美韩、美菲、美澳等一系列海上联演等。这其中既有例行性海上联演,也有特殊意义的海上联演,但无论是何种联演,参与联演的每一方都有着自己参与和实施的深层考虑。

从演习难度和强度上看,目前各国军队均积极应对世界新军事变革挑战,加大战略调整力度。因此有关专家预言,未来世界各国军队的海上联演形式将与战争样式越来越呈现趋同化,随着国际安全合作的不断深化,海上联演新的发展趋势已初露端倪。

一是演习内容进一步拓展，安全合作从传统安全领域向非传统安全领域扩大。海上联演不再局限于加强传统军事合作、巩固军事同盟关系。越来越多的国家为了有效应对新的安全威胁，致力于通过联演提高开展国际协作、共同控制危机的能力，演习内容向着打击恐怖主义、开展灾害救援等非传统安全领域合作进一步扩展，打击跨国犯罪、开展联合扫毒、遏止生态危机等更加频繁地成为联演演练的科目。

二是演习手段进一步创新，各国逐渐把一些先进的训练手段应用到海上联演中。随着计算机网络技术的日趋成熟和各国军队作战模拟水平的不断提高，虚拟现实技术和作战模拟技术将成为联演的重要技术手段，一体化网上联合作业将成为联演的重要形式。海上联演指挥正从协同型向一体化发展，演习编组也从独立编组向混合编组转变，演习保障从自我保障向联合保障转变，以实现优势互补和功能聚合，提高演习效益。

三是演习影响进一步扩大，海上联演目的在于获取政治、外交、军事、经济等多方面的综合战略利益。海上联演具有很强的政治性、战略性，作为军队和平时期对外交往的重要形式，它是各国运筹国际关系、经略周边环境、维护国家利益的战略举措，是各国开展互动交流、增强安全互信的重要舞台。各国将进一步加强对海上联演的运筹谋划，以不断提高参演国家的政治影响力、军事互信度，强化演习的外交功能。

此外，建立常态化演习项目或机制，建立通用作业规范、标准流程等均是未来海上联演的发展趋势。

89. 海上联演怎样解读新装备发展现状与趋势？

首先，很多海上联演都着力展示参演国最新的海上武器装备，以期达到多重效果，目的之一便是通过演习检验新式武器装备的作战性能，这也是从海上联演中解读新装备发展趋势的较好途径。

其次，从演习效果的评估中看，海上联演不仅是参演国展示武力的手段，也是各国发现自身作战能力不足之处的途径。面对演习中出现的短板，不难预料到针对这些短板而出现改进或者创新的新装备发展趋势。

90. 海上联演需要在哪些方面重点加强？

一是迫切需要制定海上联演法规，使联演有法可依。随着国家发展战略和安全战略的贯彻落实，国家战略利益将不断拓展，组织和参与海上联演已逐步成为常态。海上联演涉及面广、政策性强，不少敏感问题涉及中外法律法规。从长远着想，需尽早以立法的形式对海上联演问题进行规范。

二是迫切需要建立海上联演机制，使联演直接为提高战斗力水平服务。近年来的双边或多边海上联演既促进了睦邻友好关系，扩大了国家、军队的国际影响，也为了解、学习外军提供了窗口。今后要在服从政治、外交、军事战略需要的前提下，重点考虑提升演习规模、层次、兵力，形成真正意义上的海上联演，为提高作战能力服务。

三是迫切需要加大军事交流的步伐，使海上联演的层次和质量有新的跃升。海上联演是军事交流的重要方式，也是学习借鉴外军联合作战、一体化训练经验的重要途径。同步重视与大国海军、强国海军及周边邻国海军进行海上联演，吸纳各家之长，不断提高与各国海军联演的能力。

91. 海上联演怎么应对未来海上多样化安全威胁？

海上联演会根据不同的时代背景被赋予不同的任务。联演逐步转变为和扩大到加强地区海上力量合作、共同维护海上安全等方面，联演科目也从传统的联合作战逐步扩大到非传统安全领域，包括人道主义救援减灾、医疗救灾以及反海盗等。

92. 海上联演人才队伍怎么建？

一是重视海上联演人才教育。把海上联演方面的素质教育培养贯穿军官成长的全过程，根据任命前、初级、中级、高级等级别，对应到不同级别院校或培训班中进行。把海上联演人才队伍建设摆在战略位置，做实育才、引才、聚才、用才工作，培养大批高素质新型人才。特别是院校作为人才培养源头，需瞄准世界一流标准建校育人，以更为宽阔的视野、更加强烈的使命担当，夯实人才基石。

二是建立一支专门从事海上联演教育的高素质教官队伍。搞好海上联演教育的关键是建设一支高素质的教官队伍。为此，从事海上联演教育的教官一般要求有硕士或博士学位，具有筹划组织或参加联演的经历，各军兵种人数大致相当，其中大多数应接受过高级联合职业军事教育。

三是加强对外军事交流与合作。随着海军战略转型，海军战略性、综合性和国际性军种属性不断突显，对海军官兵的国际素养提出了更高要求。院校必须把学员国际化素养培育作为人才培养的重要环节。要加大开放办学的力度，注重拓宽对外交流合作的渠道，深化内外训互动交流，丰富学员国际化素养的实际经历体验。要拓展航海实习环节，通过实地参与、综合演练等途径，掌握海上国际公约、外交礼仪和应急处置方法。要扩大"走出去"的人员数量和整体规模，增强培训任务和人员选派的科学性、计划性，真正用世界眼光来培育高素质创新型人才。一方面培养掌握多种能力的复合型人才。例如，既懂军事又懂管理、既懂指挥又懂技术、既懂海军又懂陆空军、既懂军种作战又懂联合作战、既具有国际视野又熟悉外军的复合型人才；另一方面培养具有较强外语交流能力的人才。这有利于通过扎实有效的外事活动和周密细致的组织协调，保证海上联演各方紧密配合、意图准确沟通、演习成效明显，做到协调有力、沟联顺畅、保障高效，产生外交、政治、军事等综合效应，展示军队、海军的良好形象。

93. 院校在海上联演人才培养方面应发挥什么作用？

当前，各国军队相互"交流"的机会越来越多，其中参加海上联演是重要方式之一，海上联演也是和平时期各国海军部队提高一体化联合作战能力最直接、最有效的途径。因此，培养海上联演师资力量也成了各国海军客观存在的需求。优质的师资力量有利于查找在一体化联合作战能力方面存在的缺陷和不足，提出指导性意见，从而使今后的演训对症下药，有的放矢，更有利于推进演训工作扎实有效地进行。

一是搞好顶层设计，发挥政策法规"模具"效应。从顶层设计入手，根据海上联演特点，由机关与各层级部队共同商议，熔铸相关军事文化，建立统一的海上联演训练体系，出台权威性的海上联演师资力量培养相关政策法规，通过制度不断完善海上联演师资的层次，使海上联演人才培养标准化、体系化。

二是让院校教员到一线参加海上联演。为了提高遂行海上一体化联合行动任务的能力和水平，要对参与任务的部队进行不同种类、不同层次和不同规模的军事训练。在实际的海上联演和模拟训练中，应当让院校的军事研究、战略指挥、外事交流等方面的教员充分参与其中，这样在有充分理论基础的情况下，也能够通过实践进一步提升理论素养，为后期的海上联演人才培养奠定坚实的基础。

三是加强海上联演思维模式的塑造，培养联合作战人才。在联演师资力量的培养过程中，充分体现融入一体化的"联演联训"，摒弃"单军种"作战观念，培养联演思维模式。可以给受训人才安排角色的切换，有时充当演训的组织者，有时是演训的保障者，有时是具体实践者，他们所接受的一体化联合战役战术训练，既有理论，又有实践，是全方位的教育训练。

94. 海上联演新闻报道未来的发展方向有哪些？

一是聚焦异国认知差异，树立跨文化的传播意识。随着网络技术的飞速发展，信息的即时传输和网络的无国界化使海上联演宣传从国内宣传、对外宣传两条路转变为内外宣传合二为一，这也会对新闻报道提出实施跨文化传播战略的要求。树立跨文化传播意识，要挖掘边际信息。军队形象建构，如果内容指向性太强，仅仅涉及与形象直接相关的信息，难以引起公众的兴趣。如果能注重挖掘公众爱看的与军队形象相关或者暗含军队形象的故事，从外围培养军队的认知度和美誉度，增强传播内容的可读性、趣味性，往往能取得意想不到的效果。此外还应充分利用媒体"走出去"，海上联演的报道，要拓展报道语言，报道语种应包含恰当的中文、英语、阿拉伯语、俄语、法语、西班牙语等大语种的语言，积极掌握话语权，以防被外国媒体和外国受众误读误解。

二是重视军队文化交流，打造友好名片。加强军队对外文化交流，充分利用海上联演收尾之际的文化活动，打造和谐友好的印象，用文化这张"名片"敲开世界的心扉。在海上联演收尾之际，参演军队开展拔河、足球、篮球及乒乓球等丰富多彩的文体交流活动。在活动结束后，各国参演官兵可组织策划一些喊口号或举横幅之类的小花絮，或准备拿手的文艺节目，在海上联演之后向外军展示我国、我军的文化。在文化活动期间，还可以邀请一些国际友人上舰围观赛况，见证友谊，并可通过民间传播渠道使海上联演报道更加丰满。

三是重视媒体平台建设，使传统媒体与新媒体融合发力。在当今社会，军队媒体仅占有"权威"信息是不够的，要充分利用新兴媒体，尽可能多地占有传播渠道和发布"权威"信息的强大媒体平台，让海上联演的"权威"信息被尽可能多的人获悉和认可。海上联演报道要强化互联网思维，遵循新闻传播规律和新兴媒体发展规律，坚持发挥传统媒体的信誉优势，及时发布权威信息和辟谣信息，并且适度选择运用网络语言，增加海上联演报道的趣味性和可读性；与此同时，要发挥以微博、微信为代表的新兴媒体的传播优势和技术优势，提高海上联演报道的即时性、直观性、互动性，使受众对海上联演报道的印象从平面走向立体、从被动接受走向主动参与。

95. 海上联演与未来海上作战样式有何相关？

未来的海上作战已经转到现在的高科技方向。通过海上联演可以先期对构想的作战方式进行检验并作出改正，以便在未来的战场上获得更多主动权。

96. 海上联演将来是否会邀请更多国家参加？

对于以政治意味为主的海上联演，各国的姿态会更加开放和透明，参与度也会更高，有利于促进世界和平进程。但对于有些含有军事高级机密、核心技术的海上联演还是会以结盟国为主，以此来保护本国的军事实力和军事信息，不会轻易邀请他国，特别是潜在对手。

97. 如何提升海上联演对海军战斗力建设的贡献度？

海上联演对促进海军部队战斗力建设具有明显作用。各国进行海上联演有助于提高联合行动下的组织、协调、保障能力，完善、优化各方海上联演的组织方法。组织和参加海上联演是运筹国际关系、经略周边环境、维护地区和平与稳定、展示国威军威、促进部队战斗力建设的重要举措，可以在以下几个方面进一步加深和拓展。

一是加大与外国海军举行海上联演的复杂程度。在演习科目设置上不局限于搜救、损管、编队运动等简单科目，逐步增加舰炮攻击、扫布雷等复杂科目。在演习想定设置上立足实战，锻炼部队在真实和复杂条件下应对突发事件的能力，从实战出发，促进海军战斗力建设。在演习涉及领域上，逐步扩展到人道主义救援、反恐等非传统安全领域的海上联演。

二是探索实现海上联演的机制化和海上联演的多种模式。对于重点方向，尝试实现海上联演的机制化，定期举行海上联演。在海上联演模式上更为灵活，除了实兵演习，还可以采取兵棋推演、室内研讨会、相互邀请参加和观摩对方演习等多种方式。

三是着眼于学习外军先进技术经验，重点加强联合指挥和通信方面的训练。外国海军在装备、训练、技术等方面有许多值得借鉴，特别是在指挥程序和通信文件方面，以美国为主制定的《演习战术1000》系列条令等北约演习指挥和通信文件，系统规范，可操作性强，值得借鉴，并应在今后演习中进行针对性的训练，进一步加强与外国海军的联合指挥、协同和通信能力。

98. 新形势将对组织和参与海上联演提出什么新的要求？

一是适应国家海洋权益新拓展，展露决心意志。海洋强国是指在开发海洋、利用海洋、保护海洋和管控海洋等方面拥有强大综合实力的国家。我国提出建设海洋强国的战略目标，既是着眼于中华民族的伟大复兴，也是着眼于我国海洋权益的维护。为了维护国家的主权和领土完整，维护国家的发展利益，海军在海洋上的维权力度也将不断增大。因此，需要通过海上联演，彰显我国维护地区及世界和平与稳定的坚定决心，展露保护国家发展利益的坚强意志，震慑国内外敌对势力，展示我军威武之师、文明之师的形象。另外，通过海上联演，可以学习借鉴外军维护国家海洋权益的有益经验，锻炼摔打部队，提高我国海军核心作战能力和应对多种安全威胁以及完成多样化军事任务的能力。

二是践行人类命运共同体新理念，展现大国担当。2017年3月17日，联合国安理会一致通过的第2344号决议，首次载入"构建人类命运共同体"这一重要理念。从近现代国际关系的历史经验来看，大国在走向国际舞台中心的过程中，必然伴随着承担更多国际责任的内在要求和外在需要，如果不能积极参与国际事务，帮助国际社会解决实在问题，是很难赢得其他国家的尊重和认可的。海军作为国际性、战略性、综合性军种，是国际责任担当的重要力量，在海洋空间践行"人类命运共同体"新理念中发挥着不可替代的重要作用。在传统安全领域，通过海上联演这一特殊的多边合作形式，使世界各国走近中国军队，了解中国军队，对外显示我军对地区稳定、世界和平的作用价值。同时，针对非传统安全威胁跨国性、连锁性、扩散性等特点，通过拓展海上联演内容样式，弘扬人道主义，建立多边安全对话机制，从而对在捍卫世界和平、推动共同安全建设、促进军事文化交流做出独特贡献，彰显大国担当。

三是服务国家"一带一路"新倡议，展示合作诚意。"一带一路"中的"21

世纪海上丝绸之路"倡议希望通过政策沟通、设施联通、贸易畅通、资金融通、民心相通，建立全方位的蓝色伙伴关系，推进海上互联互通，实现共同发展。在这个过程中，各海洋国家需要加强各领域特别是海上的安全合作，共建"海洋命运共同体"，为沿岸国家经贸领域合作及发展保驾护航。"21世纪海上丝绸之路"倡议所蕴含的深层次人文理念，有助于弱化地区安全交往中的敏感问题，海上联演可以展示合作诚意，推动地区合作协商机制的发展，更好地促进沿线国家的贸易往来。

99. 新形势下发展海上联演的基本理念是什么？

一是突破传统思维，以创新谋求新发展。进入21世纪以来，我国多次运用海上联演这一方式，取得了外交领域的重大突破，不但丰富了我国的外交思想，拓宽了传统的外交渠道，而且显示了我国高超的外交智慧。当前，国际战略格局深刻演变，国家利益向海外拓展迅速，海军走向远洋的机遇和挑战并存。因此，必须牢固树立创新理念、前瞻理念和超越理念，确保海上联演始终能够服务于国家经略海洋的大政方针，有利于推动和谐海洋构建的美好愿景。树立创新理念，就是打破经验主义的束缚，不能走老路，也不能罔顾国情军情，亦步亦趋，盲目生搬硬套外军组织海上联演的做法。树立前瞻理念，就是要着眼于服务国家战略，形成常态化、机制化海上联演模式。树立超越理念，就是要用发展的眼光布局海上联演的形式和内容，并按阶段有步骤地推进，使之与国家发展和军队建设的进程相配合、相衔接。

二是构建和谐海洋，拓展军事外交职能。海上联演作为国际海上军事安全合作的重要形式，既要着眼于本国海洋战略目标的实现，也要有助于国家和谐海洋环境的营造，构筑海上持续安全的稳定机制。通过海上联演促进各国关系的发展，仍然是外交领域的一种新样式。要通过创新海上联演形式和内容，积极拓展军事外交职能，持续稳定地发挥自身在国际上的战略影响力。与发展海军硬实力相比，提升国际战略影响力是更加重要的课题，也是建设一流海军的应有之义。新形势下通过多种形式海上联演，表达我国积极履行国际义务,加强海洋安全合作,参与全球海洋治理的愿望;不断提升自己在参与国际事务中的能力,为维护世界海洋和平以及构建海洋命运共同体持续发挥积极作用。

三是维护地区安全,发挥积极作用。海上联演不仅是提高部队战斗力的一种手段,而且是对外传递政治信息的一种途径。随着我国经济的高速发展,我国与东南亚各国在政治、经济、文化等多个领域的合作不断加深和拓展。《中国的军事战略》白皮书也明确提出,将通过"加强海外利益攸关区国际安全合作,维护海外利益安全"。自20世纪末以来,东南亚成为世界海上恐怖活动最为严重的地区,马六甲海峡也成为全球五大海上恐怖活动多发区之一。因此,东南亚国家海上联演的广泛开展,在一定程度上有助于东南亚国家之间以及东南亚国家与区外大国之间增信释疑、深化友好。例如,新加坡、马来西亚和印度尼西亚三国之间长期开展多边海上联演。近年来,中国、泰国开展的"蓝色突击"海军陆战队联合演训不仅深化了中泰之间的战略互信,也向其他东南亚国家展示了中国和谐海洋理念,有利于中国与东南亚国家加强相互尊重与理解,消弭误解和矛盾,发展睦邻友好的互信伙伴关系。

100. 新形势下海上联演创新发展有哪些着力点?

一是发展海上联演对象与形式。海军无论是作为国家利益的捍卫者,还是作为国际海上秩序的维护者,都离不开国际合作。对我国海军而言,一方面要积极拓展海上联演对象,开展同印度、新加坡、马来西亚、印度尼西亚以及中东国家的海上联演。既要实现海上军事力量与优势的互补,保持海上航道的安全与畅通,避免海盗、恐怖分子的侵扰。另一方面,要探索发展海上联演形式,积极推进与东盟国家海军对话机制,组织与东盟海上联演,有效加强海上安全合作,增加互信,提升共同应对安全威胁的能力。

二是深化海上联演的内容。在继续举行海上联演,加大对海上合作安全机制探索力度的基础上,应积极探索在未来组织、参与海上联演的实践中，提升联演层次，着重在丰富联演内容、扩大联演规模、完善联演机制等方面下功夫。前期可以通过海上联演加强与各国海上行动层面的交流，以联合巡逻为形式，以共同执法为内容，为我国构建更为广泛的多边海上合作机制奠定技术基础，构筑行动框架。

三是制定完善的海上联合军事行动战术规则。当前，应加强对海上联演机制化、常态化的研究，力争建立一个或数个以中国为东道国的、有中国特色的、机制化、成系统的海上联演体系，探索实现海上联演的机制化和模式多样化，这些都需要成熟、完善的海上联合军事行动规则的规范和牵引。军事行动战术规则是本国或本国与他国间，以条文的形式规定军队各类人员及武器装备的职责、义务和规范化战术行动的指令。当今世界上的现代化军队，特别是美国、英国等西方国家军队，在海上联合军事行动方面都有各自一套比较完善的兵力行动战术规则指令，包括《海军基本战术技术规则》《海军通信规则》《多国海上联合行动规则》《海军作战保障后勤与装备规则》《非战争行动规则》等。这些条令性文件通过指南、手册和词典等形式，以程序性和规则性条文详细规定了各类人员及各种武器装备在海上军事行动中的职责、义务和规范化的战术行动程序，从技术层面上非常利于各国海军舰艇统一操作程序。实际上，我国海军在参与海上联演中已经开始接触一些外军的军事行动战术规则，加强了双方兵力之间的了解，取得了很好的效果。

附 录

附录1

国外重大海上联演概览

军演名称代号	演习时间	演习海域	参演国家	演习概况
环太平洋联演	2016年6—8月	夏威夷群岛海域、加利福尼亚海域	美国、英国、加拿大、澳大利亚、新加坡、菲律宾等25国	"环太平洋"联演(Rim of the Pacific, RIMPAC)是由美国主导的世界上规模最大的多边海上联合演习。自1971年开始,至苏联解体前,每年举行一次;苏联解体后,每两年举行一次。目的在于保障太平洋沿岸国家海上通道的安全以及联合反恐。"环太平洋-2016"军演有25国、46艘舰船、5艘潜艇、200架飞机以及25 000人员参演(摘自《科技日报》2016年7月24日第2版)
"卡拉特"海上联合战备训练	2017年5月	南海	美国、泰国、马来西亚、新加坡、菲律宾等9国	"卡拉特"海上联合战备训练演习(Cooperation Afloat Readiness and Training, CARAT)主要科目有水面作战、反潜、防空、两栖攻击、特种作战、实弹射击以及助民活动等。"海上联合战备训练-2017"有9国、50余艘舰船参演,自1995年起每年一届,是美国海军在南亚和东南亚进行的历史最久远的地区演习(摘自共同社2017年6月24日电)
"马拉巴尔"联演	2017年6月	印度洋	美国、印度、日本	"马拉巴尔"联演(Malabar)原本是美印之间常态性的年度演习。美印两国从1993年开始每年都会举行"马拉巴尔"联合军事演习,印度在1998年进行核试验后,军演一度中断,但从2002年再度恢复。日本于2007年首次参加,并于2015年正式成为参演国。"马拉巴尔-2017"有3国、10余艘舰船参演(摘自《和平与发展》2017年第5期)

续附表

军演名称代号	演习时间	演习海域	参演国家	演习概况
"动态猫鼬"联演	2017年6—7月	大西洋北部区域	挪威、加拿大、法国、德国、爱尔兰、英国等10国	"动态猫鼬"联演（Dynamic Mongoose）是北约领导的年度海上反潜战互操作性演习，是北约两个年度反潜训练之一，每年一次。北约于2017年6—7月在大西洋举行了"动态猫鼬-2017"演习，演练了如何对付潜在敌人的潜艇。共有10国、2000余人、5艘潜艇、11艘水面舰艇和8架海军直升机参演[摘自《人民日报》（海外版）2017年6月18日讯]
"动态蝠鲼"联演	2017年3月	中地中海	意大利、法国、希腊、西班牙、土耳其、美国、加拿大、德国、挪威等10国	"动态蝠鲼"联演（Dynamic Manta）是北约领导的年度海上反潜战互操作性演习，是北约两个年度反潜训练之一，每年一次。"动态蝠鲼-2017"有10国、10艘军舰参演[摘自《人民日报》（海外版）2017年3月11日讯]
"海上微风"联演	2017年7月	黑海	美国、乌克兰、北约国家	"海上微风"多国联演由乌美两国于1997年发起，后发展为年度例行军演，通常持续两周左右。2017年7月10—22日，由乌克兰和美国主导的"海上微风-2017"多国联演在乌克兰南部的黑海海域举行，更有乌克兰、美国、加拿大、法国、英国、土耳其、瑞典等16个国家，近30艘舰船、22架飞机、近100辆装甲车参演。期间，多国海上司令部根据演习指令进行战术规划和兵力调遣，加强各国间海上和空中力量的协同作战技术（摘自央广网2017年7月11日）
"三叉戟"联演	2015年10月	地中海和东大西洋	美国及北约19国	"三叉戟-2015"联演（Trident）是北约举行冷战结束以来兵力规模最大、分布地域最广、实施难度最大、演练要素最全的演习，共有70多艘舰艇和潜艇、海上巡逻机和3000多名海军陆战队员参演，设有两栖登陆等课目，演习旨在增强部队战斗力一体化（摘自法新社2015年10月6日讯）

续附表

军演名称代号	演习时间	演习海域	参演国家	演习概况
"波罗的海行动"联演	2017年6月	波罗的海	美国与北约国家	"波罗的海行动"联演(Baltops)是美国与14个盟国和伙伴国家的50艘舰艇一起参加的大型海上联合演习,是波罗的海地区一年一度的多国海上演习,旨在提高指挥的灵活性和武器装备的操作熟练度,展示提供海上控制和项目力量的能力(摘自新华社塔林2017年6月24日讯)
"辉煌水手"联演	2017年9月	地中海	北约与法国	"辉煌水手-2017"联演(Brilliant Mariner)是北约战斗快速反应小组与法国快速反应部队应对小范围区域冲突的针对性训练,旨在加强检测三个北约常设小组与法国航空海军快速反应部队快速行动能力(摘自中华新闻网海外版2017年10月2日讯)
"鹞鹰/关键决心"联演	2017年3月	韩国本土及领海	美国、韩国	"鹞鹰/关键决心"联演(Foil Eagle)始于1994年4月,原名为"阿尔索伊"。2008年更名为"鹞鹰/关键决心"联演,是美韩三军联合训练演习。"鹞鹰-2017"联演美韩两国出动3万余士兵和10余艘舰船参演(摘自中国新闻网2017年3月13日讯)
"不屈意志"联演	2016年10月	韩国周边海域	美国、韩国	"不屈意志-2016"联演(Invincible Spirit)被认为是美韩1976年来最大规模的三军联合演习。2016年10月10—15日,美国出动7艘舰艇参演,韩国派出40多艘舰艇,内容包括反特种部队作战和精准打击陆上核心设施训练等科目(摘自新华社首尔2016年10月11日讯)
"乙支自由卫士"联演	2017年8月	韩国周边海域	美国、韩国	"乙支自由卫士"联演(Ulchi-freedom Guardian)是由美韩参联会共同协调,美太平洋总部主持,美韩联合部队司令部具体组织实施。该演习始于1976年,原名"乙支焦点透镜",2009年更名为"乙支自由卫士"。该演习为年度例行性演习,2017年有5万名韩国军人、1.75万美国军人和美第七舰队参演(摘自新华社北京2017年8月22日讯)

续附表

军演名称代号	演习时间	演习海域	参演国家	演习概况
"协作精神"联演	1993年	韩国附近海域	美国、韩国	"协作精神"联演(Team Spirit)始于1976年,从1976年到1993年共举行了17次(1992年例行演习被取消),参演兵力一度超过20万人,囊括海、陆、空及特殊军种,一度成为美国规模最大的海外军事演习。该演习于1993年起暂停,迄今没有恢复(摘自《北京日报》2014年4月30日讯)
"多路航行"联演	2017年3月	关岛海域、印度洋、西太平洋	美国、日本	"多路航行-2017"联演(Multi Sail)有美方10余艘主力军舰和日方多艘驱逐舰参加。该演习自2004年起每年一届,是美日最高规格的海上联演(摘自《中国青年报》2017年3月17日讯)
"勇敢之盾"联演	2016年9月	关岛附近海域	美国、日本	"勇敢之盾"联演(Valiant Shield)始于2006年,每两年由美军太平洋司令部在关岛附近海域举行,以两栖攻防作战为重点,包含海上安全、反潜作战、空中防卫等科目。"勇敢之盾-2016"有美日两艘航母在内的19艘军舰、180多架军机和大约1.8万名士兵参加。演习表明美国重返亚太的决心,明确并巩固了美日在亚太地区的同盟关系(摘自央广军事2016年9月15日电)
"利剑"联演	2016年10月	关岛附近海域	美国、日本	"利剑"联演(Keen Sword)是美日两军从1986年开始每两年举行一次的军事演习。"利剑-2016"联合军事演习内容包括海上支援、海上搜救、紧急提供燃料、提供弹药等演练科目。共有美军1.1万人、日军2.5万人、20艘潜艇、260架飞机参演(摘自《科技日报》2016年11月9日第6版)
美日澳海上联演	2017年6月	日本周边海域及南海	美国、日本、澳大利亚	美日澳海上联演始于2007年。"美日澳海上联演-2017"共有4艘舰艇和1艘潜艇参演,首次进入中国南海海域。演习内容包括海上通信等基础科目(摘自新华社2017年6月9日讯)

续附表

军演名称代号	演习时间	演习海域	参演国家	演习概况
"铁拳"夺岛联演	2016年1月	美国加利福尼亚海域	美国、日本	"铁拳"夺岛联演（Iron Fist）始于2006年。2016年，这一军演在美国加利福尼亚海域举行，为实兵演习。此演习是双方培养进攻作战能力、夺岛作战能力和海外部署能力的专项演习（摘自《南方日报》2016年11月14日第A11版）
"山樱"夺岛联演	2017年12月	日本东部海域	美国、日本	"山樱"夺岛联演（Yama Sakura）始于1982年，"山樱-2017"是美日第73次举行该演习。日本方面投入以陆自东北方面队为中心的5000余人，美军则有1600余人参加演习。内容包括两栖登陆、弹道导弹攻击和舰艇火力支援等科目（摘自环球网2017年12月6日讯）
"金色眼镜蛇"联演	2017年2月	泰国	泰国、美国、日本、韩国、马来西亚、中国等9个国家	"金色眼镜蛇-2017"联演（Cobra Gold）有来自美国、日本、韩国、印度尼西亚、马来西亚等27个国家共8000多名陆、海、空军方人员参加军演。该演习自1982年以来每年举行一次，是泰美共同主办的年度机制性多边联合军演（摘自新华网2017年2月13日电）
"肩并肩"联演	2016年4月	苏比克湾	美国、菲律宾、澳大利亚	"肩并肩"联演（Balikatan）是年度例行性军事演习，始于1981年，1995年中断后，1999年重新恢复。"肩并肩-2016"是第36届，在菲律宾北部吕宋岛等地举行，为期两周，澳大利亚首次参与，内容包括运输、实弹射击练习、大面积人员伤亡的救助、丛林生存训练、抢滩登陆等科目，美、菲、澳共计8000名军人参演（摘自《文汇报》马尼拉2016年4月7日专电）
"太平洋狮鹫"联演	2017年8月	太平洋海域	美国、新加坡	"太平洋狮鹫-2017"联演（Exercise Pacific Griffin）是美新两国出动护卫舰和海鹰直升机的实战合训，旨在增加综合反潜、反地面和反空作战能力，加强两军友好互通，是美国和新加坡首次海上联合军演（摘自国防部新闻中心2017年9月4日电）

续附表

军演名称代号	演习时间	演习海域	参演国家	演习概况
"乌尼塔斯"联演	2017年7月	秘鲁海域	美国、秘鲁、巴西、阿根廷、澳大利亚等19国	"乌尼塔斯-2017"联演(Unitas)在秘鲁举行,是美国在南美洲最大的海上联合军事演习,旨在加强与南美洲盟友的安全协作能力(摘自新华社利马2017年7月1日讯)
"光明星"联演	2017年9月	地中海海域	美国、埃及	"光明星"联演(Light Star)始于1981年,此前每两年举行一次。2013年,美国以埃及当局对前总统穆尔西的支持者使用暴力为由取消联演,此后一直没有恢复。特朗普就任美国总统后,埃美关系逐渐升温。2017年9月,双方重启中断多年的"光明星"联演。内容包括海空联合作战、水面搜救、突击搜查可疑船只、协调反恐训练等科目(摘自新华社开罗2017年9月10日讯)
"因陀罗"联演	2017年10月	日本海海域	印度、俄罗斯	"因陀罗"联演(Indra)原为印苏年度例行演习,苏联解体后,印俄在2003年4月举行首次"因陀罗"联演,第二次是2005年10月,在印度洋海域举行,而后2007年、2009年、2012年、2014年分别在俄罗斯符拉迪沃斯托克外海和索马里外海举行。"因陀罗-2014"内容包括联络军官交流、通信演练、海上作战群行动、直升机跨甲板登陆、射击演习、海上打击、防空演习、岸基水面打击和反潜战等科目。"因陀罗-2017"中,印度共派出350名陆军官兵、80名空军官兵、2架伊尔-76飞机以及2艘护卫舰参演;俄罗斯派出东部军区的太平洋舰队、空军和陆军部队的人员及武器装备参加演习,参演人员大约有1000人(摘自国防部2017年10月15日讯)

续附表

军演名称代号	演习时间	演习海域	参演国家	演习概况
"伐楼拿"联演	2017年4月	印度洋沿海	印度、法国	"伐楼拿"联演(Varuna)是2001年首次举行的年度性联合演习,内容包括"所有海上行动",包含航母作战、反潜战和海上拦截等科目。"伐楼拿-2017"联演为举行的第15届"伐楼拿"军演,共有6艘舰艇参演(摘自《法国印太防务战略》)
"康坎"联演	2017年5月	普利茅斯海域	印度、英国	"康坎"联演(Konkan)是自2004年起每年举行的系列演习。该演习机制灵活,桌面推演和实战演习交替进行,2006年为实战演习,在印度果阿海岸举行;2007年为桌面推演,在英国普利茅斯海战中心举行;2009年为实战演习,在英国水域举行;2010年为桌面推演;2011年在阿拉伯海举行。"康坎-2017"联演在英国举行,演习内容包括联合登船训练、近距离战斗和运送伤员科目,共有2个突击队,100余人参演(摘自《亚太海洋安全与研究》2017年第12期)

附录 2

海上联演常用英语 300 句[①]
Common English 300 for Maritime Joint Exercise

I An Introduction to Maritime Joint Exercise 海上联演概述

1. What is the purpose/intention of the maritime joint exercise? 海上联演的目的/意图是什么？

2. Would you please specify the objective/goal/mission of the maritime joint exercise? 能否具体说明一下海上联演的目标/任务？

3. The general purposes are to develop an understanding of participating navies' MCM (Mine Counter Measures) procedures, their medical and safety procedures, and to demonstrate participating navies' capabilities in MCM operations. 总目标是：了解参演国海军的反水雷战程序、医疗和安全程序，以及展示参演国海军的反水雷战能力。

4. Where is the maritime joint exercise area? 海上联演的区域在哪里？

5. What serials will be conducted in the maritime joint exercise? 海上联演将安排哪些科目？

6. Would you please show us the coordinates and reference points that indicate the maritime joint exercise area? 能否让我们看看标识海上联演区域的坐标和参考点？

7. Shall we follow the local time or the UTC (Universal Time Coordinated)? 我们是使用当地时间还是世界时？

8. Would you please provide us with the charts used for the maritime joint exercises? 能否提供海上联演用的海图？

9. The chart to be used is Admiralty Chart xx-nn. 使用的海图是英版海图 xx-nn[②]。

---

① 本附录内容为国际海军用语。
② xx 为字母，nn 为数字——编者注

10. Pre-sail conferences are scheduled on dd-mm-yy at the navy tactical school. 航渡协调会议计划于××年××月××日在海军战术学校召开。

11. OCSs (Officers Conducting the Serial) of various serials are to attend with orders of respective exercises. 各科目的执行官应携带各自负责的演习作战命令出席会议。

12. Each OCS shall submit simple yet comprehensive instructions (PRE-EX message regarding the conduct and safety issues for each of their respective events). 各科目执行官将就各自演习的实施和安全事宜提供简短而全面的说明(演练前指令)。

13. Exercise instructions/messages are to be discussed and finalized on dd-mm-yy and to be distributed amongst participants on dd-mm-yy, by respective OCSs. 演习指令将于××年××月××日付诸讨论并最后定稿, 于××年××月××日由各科目执行官发放给参演成员。

14. This document is classified confidential (releasable to participating navies only). 这份文件定为机密件(只发给参演海军)。

15. The contents of this order will not be revealed to any other country without the prior approval of the host navy. 本命令的内容未经主办国海军的许可, 不得泄露给任何无关国家。

16. The MCMEX (Mine Counter Measures Exercise) will involve surface and underwater MCM operations carried out at the designated areas of operations. 反水雷演习将包括在指定作业区实施水面和水下反水雷作业。

17. How many phases/stages does the exercise entail? 演习包括几个阶段?

18. The multinational combined task group/multilateral MCM force will conduct MCM operations in the Orange Straits and its approaches in the following phases. 多国联合特混大队/多边反水雷部队将在奥兰奇海峡及其入口处分以下几个阶段实施反水雷作业。

19. The detailed concept of the exercise is elaborated in Annex C. 演习的概念细节在附件C中予以详述。

20. The in-harbor preparation phase is followed by a structured and tactical

sea phase. 港岸准备阶段之后,有一个海上实施和战术阶段。

21. The second phase consists of at-sea serials. 第二阶段由海上系列科目组成。

22. Before the sea phase there will be a pre-sail conference and after this phase there will be a debriefing. 在海上阶段开始之前将有一个航渡协调会,这个阶段完成后将召开情况汇报会。

23. Will the sea phase continue if the weather and sea states do not permit? 如果天气和海况条件不允许,海上阶段还要继续进行吗?

24. We have put aside one day as a stand-by date for each phase in the event of foul weather and rough sea, or some unexpected accident. 我们为每个阶段留出一天作为机动日,以应对恶劣天气和风浪,或者意外事故等情况。

25. Participating units will arrive pm 4 July at ××× harbor or anchorage area. 参演部队将于7月4日下午到达×××港或锚地。

26. Units of visiting countries will sail am 14 July as per their assigned missions. 来访国的部队将根据所分配的任务于7月14日上午起航。

27. The tactical phase will commence/begin/be initiated on 11 August with the MCMTA (Mine Counter Measures Tasking Authority) tasking of the MCM force in response to the EXCON (Exercise Control) scenario. 战术阶段将于8月11日开始,首先由反水雷任务指挥部根据演习控制官给出的战术想定为反水雷部队分派任务。

28. This phase will come to an end/be terminated/conclude with a declaration of FINEX. 这个阶段将随着演习结束命令的下达而结束。

29. All participants will return to ××× harbor on declaration of FINEX (Finish Exercise). 演习结束命令一下达,所有参演舰艇将返回×××港。

30. A GO FAST attack serial has been arranged after departure from ××× harbor in the anchorage area on 10 September 20××. 已安排于20××年9月10日离开×××港后在锚地实施快速目标攻击科目。

31. A surface firing serial has been planned in the sea phase of the exercise. 计划在演习的海上阶段执行水面射击科目。

32. Media coverage will be provided by the Public Relations Officer of the Host Navy. 由主办国海军的公共关系军官提供媒体报道事宜。

33. HMS ××× will conduct COMTRIALS (Communication Trials) with all units from 1000hrs to 1200hrs on 09 and 10 September 20××. "×××"号军舰将于20××年9月9日和10日两天的1000时至1200时，与所有部队进行通信校验。

34. Visiting ships with organic helo are to ensure that DIPCLEAR (Diplomatic Clearance) has been acquired for helo operations within the host nation's territorial waters for the period of the maritime joint exercise. 搭载舰载飞机的来访舰艇必须保证已经获得外交许可，允许直升机于演习期间在东道国领空飞行。

35. It should be noted that this is a separate diplomatic clearance (DIPCLEAR) from that required for ships and may be pursued through routine diplomatic channels. 请注意，这是一种与舰艇不同的独立外交许可，可通过常规外交途径申请。

36. Refer to Annex × for the Sea Exercise Program. 海上演习计划可参看附件×。

37. The fly past practice is a rehearsal for VVIP review. 飞行通过演练是为高官检阅安排的预演。

38. The observers and riders will embark on their assigned ship at 0900hrs. 观察员和观摩人员将于0900时登上指定的舰艇。

39. The other ships will proceed to the rendezvous (RV) point from the anchorage. 其他舰艇将从锚地驶往汇合点。

40. The VVIP will review the multinational fleet on the replenishment ship. 贵宾将搭乘补给舰检阅多国舰队。

41. The Sea Exercise Plan will be promulgated prior to the departure of the participating ships for the sea phase. 海上演习计划将于参演舰艇离港进行海上演习之前颁布。

42. The Medical Program and associated events are spelt out as at Annex ×. 医疗演练计划及相关活动在附件×中已明确给出。

43. Do we have any opportunity to learn about each other's capabilities? 我们有机会了解彼此的装备性能吗？

44. A detailed program for each nation to brief their capabilities during the in-harbour phase can be found in Annex ×. 在附件×中可以找到各国在港岸阶段介绍各自装备性能的详细计划。

45. The exercise area of operations is defined/enclosed/bounded/demarcated by the following four groups of coordinate. 演习作业区由以下四组坐标划定。

46. The exercise area is divided into four sectors. 演习区被划分为四个区域。

47. Light wind of up to 10 knots can be expected in the area. 该海区可能有风速为10节的轻风。

48. Tidal stream sets generally towards SE and NW, up to 3 knots. 潮汐流向一般为东南和西北，流速可达3节。

49. Prevailing wind direction is variable/southeast. 盛行风方向不定/东南。

50. In this area, sound is propagated at the velocity of 1544 meters per second in theater. 在该海区，声音在水中的传播速度是每秒1544米。

51. There are fishing activities in the area, which should be concentrated after sunset and prior to sunrise. 该海区有渔船活动，大多集中在日落后和日出前这段时间内。

52. The bottom of sea is mainly composed of sand and mud. 海底主要由泥沙构成。

53. About 30% of the sea bottom area is strewn with coral reefs and rocks. 海底大约30%的区域散布着珊瑚礁和暗礁。

54. As the sea bottom of the area is mainly of types A and B, with some patches of C and D, it will be favorable for mine-hunting operations. 由于该海区海底主要是A类和B类海底，有小面积的C类和D类海底，这将有利于猎雷作业。

55. Precipitation is rare, with visibility extending up to 8 nautical miles and expected sea state 1-2. 降水稀少，能见度可达8海里，预期海况1~2级。

56. The sea state is between calm and sea state 2, thus making it favorable for diving activities. 海况在平静和 2 级海况之间，有利于潜水活动。

57. Fishing nets are used and these are marked with some unlit white and blue buoys. Therefore, visual detection is extremely difficult. 有渔网，以不发光的白色和蓝色浮标做标记，目力难以检测。

58. Many of the fishing nets laid by the fishing vessels can extend up to 2 nautical miles each. 渔船布设的渔网可长达 2 海里。

59. More precise meteorological data from meteorological services will be available two days before exercise. 将于演习开始前两天提供气象服务部门的更准确气象资料。

60. The EXCORS Exercise Coordinators are responsible for the overall planning and execution of the MCMEX. 演习协调官全面负责反水雷演习的计划和执行。

61. The EXCOR coordinates and advises the tasking of participating forces through the MCMTA coordinators for the duration of the exercise. 演习协调官在演习期间始终通过反水雷任务指挥部的协调官对参演部队的任务进行协调并提供咨询。

62. The MCMTA coordinators are responsible to the EXCOR for the timely and efficient on conduct and management of all tactical operations. 反水雷任务指挥部协调官对演习协调官负责，保证及时有效地实施和组织所有的战术行动。

63. The MCMTA coordinators are responsible to the EXCOR for the tasking of the units through the respective national coordinators. 反水雷任务指挥部协调官对演习协调官负责，通过各国协调官为部队分配任务。

64. The MCMTA will be embarked onboard the LST (Landing Ship Tank) (command platform) operating off the Eastern island. 反水雷任务指挥部将设在坦克登陆舰(指挥平台)上，该舰在东岛附近海面活动。

65. Participating forces will be placed under the command and control of their respective National Coordinator throughout the exercise. 参演部队在演习全过程中都将接受本国协调官的指挥与控制。

66. The respective National Coordinator is responsible for the operational control of their ships and organic armaments throughout the exercise. 各国的国家协调官负责在演习全过程中对各自的舰艇及建制武备实施作战控制。

67. The Chief EXCON will monitor the progress of the exercise and apprise the EXCOR of the development in the exercise minefields. 演习总控制官将监控演习进程，并向演习协调官通报各演习雷区的进展情况。

68. In the COMPLAN (Communication Plan), you can find a list of contact numbers of participating forces, including their international call signs, pennant numbers, INMARSAT (International Maritime Satellite) voice numbers and INMARSAT fax/numbers. 在通信计划中，可以看到一份参演部队联系号码清单，其中包括各部队的国际呼号、舰旗号码、国际海事卫星话路号码和传真/电传号码。

69. In the conduct of the serials, units are to set watch on designated circuits 30 minutes prior to the serial start time to establish communication. 在实施各科目演练时，各部队须于科目开始前30分钟在指定线路对表，以便建立通联。

70. Sum-Check digits are to be used for all positions, bearings, courses, speeds, and frequencies, and DTG (Date Time Group) should be used in the text. 在发送舰位、方位、航向、航速和频率的时候，应使用和数校验码，文本中应使用日期时间组码。

71. The receiving operator is to ensure the check sums are correct before acknowledging the transmission. 接收方报务员必须验证和数校验码，确认正确以后，再回复收悉。

72. I assume command as OTC (Officer in Tactical Command). 我担任战术指挥官。

73. Comply with my message. 请执行我的电文指令。

74. Commence run from ahead/astern. 从队首/队尾开始本轮出击。

75. Run is completed/will be repeated/will cease. 本轮出击已完成/将重复执行/将停止。

76. Exercise is abandoned/being conducted/cancelled/completed/postponed/

resumed now/cease now/commenced now. 演习被放弃/正在执行/被取消/完成/被推迟/现在恢复/现在停止/现在开始。

77. Exercise independently. Remain within radar /VHF(Very High Frequency)/visual signaling range of this unit. 独立演习，保持在我的雷达/甚高频/视觉信号作用范围之内。

78. Tactical maneuvers by flag hoist are to commence now. 开始用信号旗指挥战术机动。

79. Fire explosive signal charges. 发射信号弹。

II Medical and Logistic Support Operations 医疗及后勤保障演练

80. The National Medical Support Teams will provide organic medical support for their own ships according to their own SOPs (Standard Operating Procedures), but will consult the EX Medical Staff for all evacuation requirements. 各国医疗保障队伍将根据本国标准操作程序为本国舰艇提供建制医疗保障，但是，如果需要转移伤病员，则必须与演习医疗保障组协商。

81. Although injuries and illnesses of any kind can be anticipated in all phases of the exercise, special considerations must be given to the following: blast injuries from demolition work, DCI (Decompression Illness) injuries in divers, trauma due to accident, acute medical or surgical operations. 虽然在演习的各个阶段都有可能发生各种伤病，但是必须特别注意以下几种情况：爆破作业造成的爆炸损伤、潜水员减压病、事故造成的外伤、内科急症或外科手术。

82. All life or limb threatening injuries will be evacuated according to the evacuation plan spelt out below. 一切危及生命或肢体的伤员均将根据下述计划实施转移。

83. Non-urgent injuries will be treated and managed by the National Medical Support Team onboard their ships or transferred to the Second Echelon of medical care for management. 非急症伤员将由各国医疗保障队在舰上就地医治，或转移到第二医疗梯队进行处置。

84. The primary Heli-CASEVAC (Helicopter-Casualty Evacuation) plan will be performed by naval SAR (Search and Rescue) assets located at Orange Naval Airbase. 主要的直升机转运伤病员计划将由位于奥兰奇海军航空兵基地的海军搜救飞机执行。

85. All DCI cases diagnosed as urgent or severe will be treated on-site with the ships organic hyperbaric chamber. 被确诊为急重减压病的病员应就地进入本舰配备的建制高压氧舱进行治疗。

86. If the ship does not have an organic chamber, the casualty will be brought to the nearest platform with a hyperbaric chamber and National Medical Support Team for immediate therapeutic recompression. 如果本舰未配备建制高压氧舱，应将伤员就近送往配备有高压氧舱和本国医疗保障队的舰艇平台，立即进行压力恢复治疗。

87. The affected ship will provide the EX Medical Staff with the following information in the event that an injury is sustained: number and identity of casualties, diagnosis and treatment rendered, type of evacuation requested (Sea or Helo), urgency of evacuation. 一旦发生人身伤害，伤员所在舰艇必须向演习医疗保障组报告以下信息：伤员人数和身份、诊断结果和处置方法、所需转移手段(海上或直升机)、转移紧迫程度。

88. The respective national representatives will be responsible for all administrative issues involved in the medical care of their personnel (e.g. informing next-of-kin, insurance, costs of treatment etc.). 各国国家代表将负责处理与本国人员医疗有关的各种行政事宜(例如，通报近亲、保险、医治费用等)。

89. National Logistic Coordinators may consider the use of any bilateral support arrangements between participating nations for their provision of logistic support to their respective units. 各国国家后勤协调官可考虑在参演国之间安排双边保障计划，为各自部队提供后勤支援。

90. All the necessary base arrangements covering entry, departure, and in-port requirements will be managed by the base liaison officer. 基地内一切事务，包括进出港和各种港内需求，将由基地联络官负责安排。

91. All units are required to submit to MCM tasking authority a Logistic Summary twice daily at 0700 hrs and 1900 hrs. The report shall include the following: fuel and water status, material state of each unit, operational availability of each unit, including weapon systems, provisioning requirements (current endurance before replenishment), personnel status, medical requirements or evacuation. 要求各部队每日两次(0700 时和 1900 时)向反水雷任务指挥部提交后勤总结报告。报告中应包括以下内容：油料及淡水状态、各部队物资状态、各部队(包括武器装备)的可利用率、食品需求(补给前的现有自持能力)、人员状态、医疗或伤病员转移需求。

92. The Ministry of Environment has strict regulations against the discharge of waste of quality beyond the standard of 20/30 near the coastal areas in this country. 环保部严禁在本国近岸海区排放质量标准超过 20/30 的污水。

93. Visiting ships that are unable to meet the standard shall contract only commercial trucks to dispose the ships' sewage and waste oil. 不能达到这个标准的来访舰艇只能联系商业车辆承包污水和废油处理业务。

III Safety at Sea 海上安全事项

94. The potential for collision at sea is very high if good and safe watch keeping is not practiced. 如果不能执行安全良好的值更瞭望制度，就非常可能发生海上碰撞事故。

95. It is highlighted that while tactical realism is desired in the exercise, safety of life and equipment overrides all other consideration. 需要特别强调的是，尽管在演习中希望达成战术真实性，但是人身安全和装备安全仍然是超越一切的考虑因素。

96. All precautions necessary to ensure the safety in operations are to be taken. These include the wearing of life-jackets by the crew at replenishment stations, putting upper decks out of bounds in heavy weather, etc. 应采取一切必要措施以保证作业安全，其中包括在补给站工作的舰员必须着救生衣，天气恶劣时上层甲板应保持无人等。

97. While the OCS will normally maneuver the formation to keep clear of shipping, occasionally it may be necessary to take positive individual evasive action to permit shipping to pass through the formation. 虽然科目执行官通常会采取全编队机动的方式远离其他船只，但偶尔也有必要主动采取单舰规避行动，以允许其他船只从编队中通过。

98. Commanding officers will maneuver independently at any time they deem necessary to avoid risk of collision. 舰长将在任何必要的时刻独立进行避碰机动。

99. This evasive action will be done without waiting for a signal to maneuver independently or waiting until an emergency develops. 不必等待独立机动信号的发出，也不必等到紧急情况发生时才执行这一规避行动。

100. The "maneuver independently to avoid shipping" signal is considered to be in force at all times. "独立机动、规避船只"的信号在任何时候均有效。

101. Measures to be taken immediately when a man falls overboard: A. Drop a life buoy. B. De-energize sweeps. C. Sound six short blasts. D. By day, hoist flag OSCAR where it can best be seen. By night, display two all round pulsating red lights arranged vertically. E. report as soon as possible to the OCS and to the ships of the formation, and inform the MCMTA immediately. 当有人落水时，必须立即采取以下措施：1. 抛出救生圈。2. 切断扫雷具电源。3. 鸣汽笛六短声。4. 昼间在最显眼处悬挂 OSCAR 旗号，夜间垂直悬挂两盏全向脉动红灯。5. 尽快向科目执行官和编队内其他舰艇通报，并立即报告反水雷任务指挥部。

102. The unit with the highest priority has the right of way. 优先级最高的单位拥有航行权。

103. The unit with higher priority has to inform those with lower priority in case of possible interference in due time. 如果可能发生干扰，享有较高优先级的单位必须适时通知优先级较低的单位。

104. When approached by another vessel, the minehunter shall signal the "U" by flashing lights and make a warning sound signal if the approaching vessel

does not take avoiding action. 当其他船只接近时，猎雷舰应通过闪光灯发出信号"U"，如果对方不采取规避动作，应发出音响信号予以警告。

105. MCM signals and lights are to be shown at all times while mine hunting and diving signals are to be shown only when diving operations are actually in progress. 在猎雷时应该始终悬挂信号和灯光标志，而只有在潜水作业实际进行的过程中才悬挂潜水信号标志。

106. Tasking authorities should order a buffer zone of at least 2000 yards between different MCM systems when they are operating simultaneously in the same objective area. 当数个反水雷系统在同一目标区同时作业时，任务指挥部应规定在不同系统之间至少保有2000码的缓冲区。

107. All attacking fighters approaching the surface force are to call on "Air Safety Circuit" before closing within 20 nautical miles of any force. 战斗机在接近水面部队时，应在进入20海里距离之前在"空中安全线路"上呼叫。

108. No live/dummy/blank ammunition is either to be used during the exercise or the actions involving use of force. 不论在演习期间，还是在动用武力时，均不得使用实弹、教练弹或空包弹。

IV Ship Maneuvering Operations 舰艇机动演练

109. A type or unit commander may, however, order a different standard tactical diameter for his ships. 然而，舰种或部队指挥官可以为属下的舰艇规定不同的标准战术回旋直径。

110. When a unit being maneuvered by its Unit Commander needs to increase speed to take or change station, the speed ordered for that unit is normally to be one knot less than stationing speed. 当编队中某部队正在根据该舰指挥官的命令加速占位或改变阵位时，为该部队下达的航速指令一般比占位航速低1节。

111. In order to facilitate station keeping, the speed at which a ship is proceeding may be indicated by small-sized numeral flags displayed from the navigation bridge or by regular-sized flags at the dip from an outboard signal halyard. 为

便于保持阵位,可在航海舰桥悬挂小型数字旗,以表明本舰当前航速;也可在舷外升降索半旗位置悬挂标准尺寸信号旗。

112. When the message orders a ship to take station in a general relative area, such as the van or real, an approximate distance may be included. Example: STATION C-1 takes station in the van at approximately 1 nautical mile. 当指令某舰前往某个相对不确定的区域去占位时(比如前卫或后卫的位置),报文中可以包含一个近似距离。例如,阵位 C-1 的意思是在前方大约 1 海里处占位。

113. Another method for ordering a station is to indicate a numbered or lettered station on a diagram. Example: STATION14…, take station14. 另外一个指示阵位的办法是指定一个带有数字或字母编号的图上阵位。例如,阵位 14……,意为占领 14 号阵位。

114. When ordered, a ship hoists DESIG followed by her station letter(s) and/or numeral(s) to confirm to the OTC that she has correctly interpreted her stationing instruction, and to indicate to adjacent ships the position to which she is proceeding, by hauling down, she indicates that she is in station. 当舰艇接收到指令后,应升起信号旗 DESIG,然后悬挂本舰阵位字母旗或数字旗,或字母加数字旗,以此向战术指挥官确认对占位命令理解正确,同时向邻近舰艇指示本舰即将前往的位置。降下此旗,则表明已经到位。

115. On arrival in station, a unit is to maintain the true bearing from its guide or indicated unit, even though its station may have been ordered by means of a relative bearing or area. 到达阵位时,即使此前得到的占位指令是以相对方位指令或区域指令的形式下达的,舰艇也必须与基准舰或指定舰艇之间保持真方位关系。

116. When the OTC signals a specific duty, such as "aircraft warning picket", to amplify the stationing signal, the performance of the assigned specific duty takes precedence over accurate station keeping. 如果战术指挥官在占位信号中附加了一个具体任务指令,如"飞机警戒哨",则应优先考虑如何执行该项任务,而不是如何精确保持阵位。

117. Commanding officers are authorized to use their discretion in handling their ships to facilitate visual signaling. A ship in line having an urgent signal to pass to the OTC or Unit Commander may haul out of line sufficiently to do so. 舰长有权决断是否需要对本舰实施机动，以便进行视觉信号通信。如果处于队列中的舰艇有必要向战术指挥官或部队指挥官发送紧急信号，可出列执行。

118. At night or in low visibility, after execution of a signaled course change, the guide of a formation may announce, "This is ×××. I am turning to port (starboard)." 在夜间或低能见度条件下机动时，当改变航向的指令被执行后，编队基准舰可宣布："我是×××舰，我舰正向左(或右)转向。"

119. The OCS will establish communications with the participating units, and order ships to rendezvous 4.5 nautical miles north of the LST by 120630 UTC. 科目执行官将与各参演部队建立通联，并命令各舰于标准时120630在坦克登陆舰以北4.5海里处会合。

120. Take station bearing 160° from the guide, distance 10 nautical miles. 在引导舰方位160°处占位，距离10海里。

121. Destroyer 3: prepare to take station as communication linking ship on bearing 250° true from ship G22, distance 20 nautical miles, to be in station by 1600hrs. 第3艘驱逐舰：准备在G22舰真方位250度，距离20海里处占位，担任通信联络舰，1600时到位。

122. Take station in the van/rear at approximately 2 nautical miles. 在队列前方/后方约2海里处占位。

123. Ships are to open from the guide and take up station. 舰艇在引导舰后方疏开占位。

124. Maintain minesweeping station astern of the next ahead. 在前行舰后方保持扫雷阵位。

125. Exchange stations with CX. 与CX舰交换阵位。

V Firing Exercises 实弹射击演练

126. Ships will fire at targets which always remain on the port bow of the firing

line to avoid possible ricochets. 为防止跳弹，舰艇射击目标总是保持在火力线的左舷舰首方向。

127. The shipboard artillery should maintain a fire rate at 1/4 of their maximum fire rate. 舰炮射速应为其最大射速的1/4。

128. The firing ship is to ensure that the range is clear up to 2 nautical miles of all vessels and divers before conducting its firing run. 在开始一轮射击之前，射击舰必须确认在靶场2海里范围内无任何舰船和潜水员。

129. The targets to be used for the live firing serial may be towing targets, free-floating targets with radar reflectors, or balloons. 实弹射击科目使用的靶标可能是拖靶、安装雷达反射器的自由漂靶，也可能是气球。

130. The exercise aims at effectively testing the impact distribution, fire rate and the probability of hitting of shipboard weapons in daylight or at night. 演习的目的是要有效地检验昼间或夜间舰艇武器的弹着点散布、射速和命中概率。

131. Within safety limits, close-in weapons may be employed to strafe at the targets for a short duration only. 只要安全许可，可利用近战武器扫射目标，但仅限于短时间内。

132. Each unit can fire at two targets according to their purpose of the drill or the assignment of ammunition. 各单位可以根据本单位的演练目的或弹药分配情况对两个目标进行射击。

133. While the firing formation is proceeding to the firing area, a situation report on the firing area will be transmitted by the screening unit. 当射击编队正在驶往射击区时，警戒部队将发送射击区情况报告。

134. The exercise will be initiated by the OTC's order to "live firing drill". This execution command to conduct live firing is consistent with the national regulations of participating countries. 战术指挥官将下令"开始实弹射击演练"，演习随之开始。这个实弹射击的执行命令与各参演国的条例是一致的。

135. Each participating unit will fire at the first floating target in the firing area, and then stop firing according to the safety regulations or ammunition allocation requirements before restarting firing at the second target. 每个参演单位将对

射击区内第一个漂靶进行射击,然后根据安全条例或由于需要配给弹药而停止射击,此后再开始射击第二个漂靶。

136. When the last run of firing is completed, all participants should remain stationary within the area of firing, disarm their weapons, and report to the OCS on completion of all these evolutions. 当完成最后一轮射击时,所有参演舰艇应在射击区内保持不动,给武器上保险,完成后向科目执行官报告。

137. Any unit unable to complete the firing should report to the OCS and proceed with the formation in the current sequential order until the entire serial is terminated. 无法完成射击的参演单位应通知科目执行官,并按现有顺序随队列前进,直至整个科目结束。

138. Flag B should be hoisted closed up throughout the duration of firing, and hauled down on other occasions. 射击全过程中,B旗升至杆顶,其他时间降下。

139. Range clearance will commence from 0830hrs to 1300hrs to ensure that the firing area is cleared of vessels before the commencement of the live firing sequence. 0830时至1300时开始靶场扫海,以确保在实弹射击开始前清空船只。

140. Range fouled by intruding vessels. 靶场不干净,有船只进入。

141. Clear the range/line of fire. 清空靶场/火力线。

142. Firing limit bearing is from ××× to ×××. 射界限制方位,自×××至×××(度)。

143. Range clear. 靶场干净。

144. Malfunctions. I have a hang fire/misfire. 故障。我舰火炮迟发火/哑火。

145. Bores clear. Five expended rounds. 炮膛检查完毕。耗弹5发。

146. The four shots of Salvo 2 landed: over 100 yards, hit, hit, and short 50 yards. 第二次齐射发落点分别为:远弹100码、命中、命中、近弹50码。

147. Target is identified/obscured/destroyed. 目标被识别/遮蔽/消灭。

148. All firings are scheduled in the morning to allow sufficient daylight hours

operations, if necessary. 如有必要，所有引爆活动都计划在上午实施，以保证充足的白昼时间进行潜水作业。

149. In the event that the ships are unable to complete the firing run, the MCMTA will designate ships for the conduct on 25 September, the standby date for the live firing of MDC (Mine Disposal Charge). 一旦不能完成该轮引爆，反水雷任务指挥部将指定舰艇于9月25日实施该科目，此为灭雷弹实弹分爆的备用日。

150. In the event of a "BLIND" or "DUD" MDC, respective national policies on countering them will be adopted. 如果发生"引信失效"或"哑弹"，则按各国条令的规定予以排除。

151. Minesweepers are requested to recover the buoyant mine cases upon sweeping the moored mine shapes. 扫雷舰在扫到练习锚雷时，应回收其漂浮雷壳。

152. Minesweepers are requested to provide an approximate datum of the swept mine and sinker to the MCMTA. 扫雷舰艇应向反水雷任务指挥部提供被扫水雷及其雷锚的大致基准。

153. This will assist the co–hosting navies in their subsequent efforts to recover the remaining sinkers. 这将有助于协办国海军随后回收剩余雷锚。

154. The ships involved are to mark the datum and recover their divers or remotely operated underwater vehicle immediately. 有关舰艇应标注基准点，立即召回潜水员或遥控水下作业艇。

155. Respective navies are to adhere to their individual stand-off ranges based on the MDC Firing Specification Table and abide by their national policies and procedures applicable in dealing with real mines and ordnance. 各国海军应根据灭雷弹实弹引爆规范表的规定，保持各自的安全距离，并按照本国处理真雷的条令和程序行事。

156. All other ships are to plot and keep clear of the enforced MDA (Mine Danger Area) unless otherwise directed by the MCMTA. 其他舰艇应标绘和远离所划定的危险雷区，除非反水雷任务指挥部另有指示。

157. If vessels are present, the firing ship will inform the CTG (Commander Task Group) and the latter will dispatch the range clearance units to inform the vessels to stay clear of the firing area. 如果靶区内有船只存在,引爆舰应报告特混编队指挥官,后者将派遣靶场扫海部队前往通知其远离引爆区。

158. In the process of preparing to fire, should any vessels be detected within the safety range, the MCMTA, the range clearance units and the firing ships will report "RANGE FOUL". 在引爆准备期间,如果反水雷任务指挥部、靶场扫海部队和引爆舰三者中任何一方发现安全距离内有船只,均应通报"靶场内有干扰目标"。

159. Once the vessel is away and the range is clear, "RANGE CLEAR" will be declared by the MCMTA and the firing ship can then resume its firing run. 当船只远离,靶场被清空时,反水雷任务指挥部将宣布"靶场内无干扰目标",此时引爆舰可恢复本轮引爆。

160. When the firing ship has successfully recovered the MDV (Mine Disposal Vehicle) or divers, she will station herself at the stand-off range to prepare for detonation. 当引爆舰成功召回水雷处置船或潜水员后,应在安全距离上占位,准备引爆水雷。

VI Communications Exercises 通信演练

161. Break Silence/Transmit on circuit indicated. 在指定线路解除静默/发射(信号)。

162. Silence lifted on acoustic/electronic emissions. 解除音响/电磁静默。

163. Use frequency switch plan CF. 启用 CF 号频率转换计划。

164. Maintain complete and continuous silence on Communication Circuit C to avoid intelligence collection from aircraft. 在通信线路 C 上连续保持完全静默,以避免情报被飞机截获。

165. I-band radar may be operated in random intervals, commencing at 1400hrs, limiting each period of operation to 5 sweeps with a maximum of 6 periods of operation per hour. 从 1400 时开始,可以不定期使用 I 波段雷达,

每个使用周期仅限扫描 5 次，每小时最多使用 6 个周期。

166. EMCON (Emission Control) PLAN EP2 is now in force in accordance with task group order. 根据特混大队命令，现在执行 EP2 号电磁控制计划。

167. The phrase "INTERCEPT OF UNAUTHORIZED EMISSION" means: this unit or unit indicated has intercepted friendly emissions which are violating silence conditions in force. 语句"截获违规发射的电磁波"意为：本部或报文注明单位截获友军违反现行静默规定发射的电磁波。

168. The phrase "EMISSION PRECAUTIONS" orders the recipient to take precautionary measures in accordance with national instructions. The purpose is to deny interception of classified information on own electromagnetic and acoustic emissions by PIC (Potential Intelligence Collector) in the area. 语句"发射防范"命令报文接收者根据本国条令采取防范措施的目的是避免本单位发射的电磁波和声波中包含的机密信息被同区域内活动的潜在情报收集者所截获。

169. This unit has intercepted enemy shipborne source radar emissions on bearing 065° on frequency of ×× MHz. 本单位截获来源于敌舰的雷达发射波，方位 065°，频率××兆赫。

170. Type of emission is fire control radar and is designated ××. 发射类型为火控雷达，型号为××。

171. Enemy is suspected of sending deceptive traffic on Circuit CA6. 怀疑敌方正在 CA6 号线路发射欺骗信息。

172. Enemy use of communications jamming countermeasures has been detected by this unit on Circuit CA4. 本部探测到敌方在 CA4 号线路使用通信干扰对抗措施。

173. Bearing of the shipborne source of emission by D/F (Direction Finding) is 076°. 测向探明，舰载发射源的方位是 076°。

174. Use electronic countermeasures against spoof. 使用电子对抗措施应对欺骗干扰。

175. It is necessary to ensure that no aircraft is present within 10 nautical miles around the area where chaff is being fired. 必须保证在箔条发射区周边 10

海里的范围内没有飞机存在。

176. A Host Navy ship (to be nominated) will be the AAWC(Anti-Air Warfare Commander) throughout the exercise. 在演习全过程，主办国海军舰艇(待任命)将担任防空作战指挥官。

177. For safety concerns, helos are not authorized to fly during ADEX (Air Defense Exercise) serials. 为保证安全，在演练防空科目期间，直升机不得起飞。

178. Height separation between various types of aircraft will be issued by the Air Safety Cell. 类飞机间的飞行高度分隔方案将由空中安全指挥组发布。

179. All attacking fighters approaching the surface force are to call on "Air Safety Circuit" before closing within 20 nautical miles of any force. 所有担任攻击的战斗机在接近水面舰艇部队的时候都必须在接近到20海里距离之前在空中安全线路呼叫。

180. Radar and communications jamming is not allowed during the exercise. 演习中不允许实施雷达和通信干扰。

181. Chaff is not to be deployed within 12 nautical miles off the coast of the Host Nation and within 30 nautical miles around the civil airport. 在主办国海岸12海里范围内和民用空港30海里范围内不得施放箔条干扰。

182. If a target unit is within 1 nautical mile of the SNIPE position, it is to be considered OOA(Out of Action), and is to take no further part in the exercise for the next 30 minutes from the time of snipe call by a unit of the other force. 如果目标单位在对方发出狙击报告时处于其狙击位置1海里范围内，即应判为"退出行动"，并于此后30分钟内不得参与演习。

VII Joint Exercises with Air Force 海空联演

183. Safety sector for friendly aircraft is Number 01, origin in the center of the force, limiting range 60 nautical miles, center bearing 120°, width 20°, limiting altitude 5000 feet, and is activated from 0800hrs to 2000hrs. 友军飞机的安全区为1号区，以编队中心为原点，限距60海里，方位中线120°，宽度20°，

限高 5000 英尺（1 英尺=30.48 厘米），有效期限 0800 时至 2000 时。

184. The threat assessed is air-launched missiles/ASM（Air to Surface Missile）-carrying aircraft/free-fall bombs/ship-launched missiles/submarine-launched missiles/torpedo bombers. 判断威胁目标为空射导弹/携带空舰导弹的飞机/自由落体炸弹/舰射导弹/潜射导弹/鱼雷轰炸机。

185. Threat is high/low from sector between 220° and 260° true. 在真方位 220°和 260°之间的扇区内有高空/低空目标。

186. I am engaging with long-range SAMs（Surface to Air Missiles）/short-range SAMs/guns/jammers. 我正在发射远程舰空导弹/近程舰空导弹/舰炮/干扰。

187. Open fire. 开火。Cease fire. 停止射击。

188. Hold fire on sector 3. 在 3 号扇区暂停射击。

189. Release decoys. Fire chaff. 发射诱饵弹。发射箔条弹。

190. No live or simulated ammunition should be used for attack. 不得用实弹或模拟弹进行攻击。

191. Engage left-hand/right-hand aircraft with medium-range SAMs. 用中程舰空导弹攻击左侧/右侧飞机。

192. Weapons free (on/in＿＿). （在＿＿方位区域）自由开火射击。

193. Weapons tight (on/in＿＿). （在＿＿方位区域）严控开火射击。

194. Missile/Aircraft splashed (shot down). 导弹/飞机被击落。

195. Friendly aircraft detected bearing 070°, distance 15 nautical miles. 发现友军飞机，方位 070°，距离 15 海里。

196. All participating units are to maintain an accurate record of all events for the purpose of hot wash up. 所有参演单位应准确记录全部活动过程，以便总结时使用。

197. Track charts, GOP (General Operational Plot), LOP (Local Operational Plot) of all interactions and narratives will be dispatched to the CTG through Los (Liaison Officers) by pm 18 August. 将于 8 月 18 日下午通过联络官把全部描述双方接触过程的航迹图、全面作战标图和局部作战标图送交特混大队指挥官。

VIII Verification, Boarding, Search and Seizure (VBSS) Operations 临检拿捕演练

198. Who is to act as the hijacked ship and who is to simulate the merchant vessel carrying vital cargoes? 谁来扮演被劫持船？谁来模拟载有重要货物的商船？

199. AOR960 will act as the hijacked ship laden with explosives and AOR966 will simulate the merchant vessel carrying vital cargoes. 960 补给舰扮演装满炸药的被劫持船，966 补给舰模拟载有重要物资的商船。

200. If any participant is unable to continue her operations due to machinery defects or otherwise, she is to indicate the nature of the defect along with the duration she is likely to remain out of action to the CTF(Commander Task Force). 如果因机械故障或其他原因，导致参演者不能继续演习行动，应向特混舰队指挥官报告故障的性质以及可能在多长时间不能参与行动。

201. The CTF will declare the particular unit "NO PLAY" and inform others accordingly. 特混舰队指挥官将宣布该单位"退出行动"并通知其他单位。

202. Empty boxes marked as "Explosives" will be embarked on the simulated merchant ship. The boxes will be stored on Deck 01 and above. 模拟商船上装载注明"炸药"的空箱子。这些箱子置于第 1 层甲板及其以上。

203. The MIO (Maritime Interdiction Operation) ship is to open out to 20 nautical miles from the simulated merchant ship in the opposite direction, remaining within her assigned area during "NO PLAY". 在"退出行动"期间，海上拦截舰应向模拟商船的相反方向展开 20 海里，但须保持在其指定责任区内。

204. Any undetected approach by a GO FAST less than 10 nautical miles from the HVU (Hijacked Vessel Unit) will be considered as successful. 若快速攻击艇已接近到距模拟被劫持船 10 海里以内，且未被发现，即可判为攻击成功。

205. The following code words will be used during the exercise: AUGUST-Exercise Temporarily Suspended; SEPTEMBER-Exercise Restarted; OCTOBER-Exercise Terminated. 演习中将使用以下代字：AUGUST——演习暂停；SEP-

TEMBER——演习重新开始；OCTOBER——演习终止。

206. Units of TG42 will be deployed in the areas bounded by the following co-ordinates. 第42特混大队所属各单位将部署在用以下坐标界定的各区域。

207. After the threat assessment, the MIO ship should close the COI (Contact of Interest) only as close as sea state and weather conditions allow. 作出威胁判断之后，海上拦截舰艇应向涉嫌目标靠拢，接近距离不得超越海况和天气条件的限制。

208. The windward side of the COI should be utilized to provide protection from possible chemical attack. 应利用涉嫌目标的向风舷一侧提供防护，防止遭到化学攻击。

209. Contact is a cargo/tanker/ferry/fishing vessel/pirate boat/potential violator/cleared vessel/hijacked vessel. 目标是货轮/油轮/渡船/海盗船/疑似违规船/清白的船只/被劫持船。

210. Assume tracking/boarding responsibility for contact. 行使对目标的跟踪/登临职责。

211. In my area I hold one unknown vessel. 在我责任区内扣留了一艘不明船只。

212. My method of boarding will be boat/helicopter. 我将用小艇/直升机登临。

213. Six short whistles should be blown in case of any malfunction on either party. All other ships involved need to make way for the ship. 双方之中任何一方如发生故障，应鸣笛六短声。其他参演舰艇须避让。

214. Either party has to alarm immediately the other party with signals of "KNOCK IT OFF" in case of serious safety concern. 如一方有重大安全顾虑，应立即发信号"KNOCK IT OFF"通知对方结束作业。

IX Landing Exercises 登陆演练

215. During the exercise, all the ships will hang "UY" International Signal Code (I'm in exercise, keep clear of me). 在演习期间，所有舰艇将悬挂

"UY"国际信号代码旗(我正在演习,请远离)。

216. Pre-H-Hour transfers are completed/dispatched. 攻击前的人员换乘已经结束/派遣完毕。

217. Pre-H-Hour transfers are delayed/advanced by hours/minutes. 攻击前的人员换乘推迟/提前小时/分钟。

218. Facilitate landing operations by moving in to thousand yards off beach. 运动至距海滩千码处,以便实施登陆作战。

219. Conduct evacuation of civilian personnel/landing force/military personnel. 实施平民/登陆兵力/军事人员转移。

220. Withdraw control groups/fire support groups/landing force/transports. 控制组/火力支援组/登陆兵力/运输船撤离。

221. The exercise covers: coordination of ship gunfire, conduct of supporting fire from boat guns, close air support; the operation of the signal communication, supply, and evacuation systems; coordination of beach and shore party activities; functioning of naval and field artillery liaison parties; manhandling of weapons and ammunition. 演习内容包括:舰炮火力协同;小艇炮火支援;近距离空中支援;信号通信、补给和转移系统作业;海滩部队和海岸部队协同动作;舰炮和野战炮联络组职能演练;人力搬运武器弹药。

222. Cooperation between army and navy components includes coordinating the activities of landing groups and boat groups, naval gunfire, field artillery and air support, naval gunfire and the advance of assault units, activities of army and navy air components, protective fires of army and navy antiaircraft and army and navy signal communication facilities and procedures. 陆海军部队的协同包括登陆部队与小艇部队间协同、海军舰炮与野战炮和空中支援间协同、海军舰炮与突击部队推进速度间的协同、陆海军空中分队协同、陆海军防空火力协同,以及陆海军通信设施和程序协同。

223. After the assembly of the joint force, training progresses through the stages requiring ships, boats and naval equipment, and cooperation of army and navy personnel. 联合部队集结完毕后,训练逐阶段展开,需要动用舰船、小艇和

海军装备，也要求陆军和海军人员之间配合行动。

224. This serial tests navy operation in getting boats into assembly and rendezvous areas, lancing to and crossing the line of departure according to schedule, and keeping the desired formation and direction of movement in the dash to the beach. 该系列科目检验小艇进入集结区和会合区，按计划到达并越过出发线，并在向海滩突击运动的过程中保持理想队形和方向等海军作战能力。

225. Landing exercises ensure that the landing force will move from ship to shore in the least vulnerable formations and arrive at the points desired in the best condition and formation for action. 登陆演习要保证登陆兵力以最不易遭受攻击的队形实施由舰到岸的运动，并以最有利于作战的条件和队形到达理想地点。

226. This training includes anti‑aircraft firing as well as firing at shore targets. 该项训练包括对空射击和对海岸目标射击。

227. During the joint training period, landing force personnel are trained in landing on the beach during daylight and darkness and in varying depths of water and surf conditions, first by single boatloads, then by boat division loads, and lastly by complete landing groups. 在联合训练期间，登陆部队人员接受昼间和夜间在不同水深和海浪条件下登上海滩的训练，首先进行单艇载人训练，然后进行艇队载人训练，最后过渡到登陆大队整体训练。

X Replenishment at Sea (RAS) Exercises 海上补给演练

228. Replenishment course is (AO) ××× (degrees). Replenishment speed (AO) ×× (knots). Ship A is to act as the control ship and the voice procedure will be used to alter course and speed. 补给航向(听令)×××(度)。补给航速(听令)××(节)。A舰担任指挥舰，利用话报通信程序改变航向和航速。

229. Form column in sequence ship A, ship B, ship C. Guide is ship A (Guided by ship A). Guide steers course ××× (degrees) at speed ×× (knots). 按照下列顺序组成纵队：A舰、B舰、C舰。引导舰是A舰。引导舰转向×××(度)，航速××(节)。

230. Ship A takes standby station on port quarter of Ship B, and Ship C is life guard and takes station 1000 yards astern of ship B. A 舰在 B 舰的舰尾左后方占领预备阵位，C 舰担任救生警戒，在 B 舰舰尾 1000 码（1 码=0.9144 米）处占位。

231. Close to me for transfer fuel at amid transfer station. 请靠近我舰，接收我舰中段补给站传送油料。

232. I have mail/light material for light line on my STBD (Starboard) side transfer. 我舰有邮件/轻型物资在右舷用灯光管制索向你传送。

233. I require diesel, quantity 500 tons/liters /gallons, by QRC (Quick Release Coupling). 我舰要求通过速开连接装置传送柴油 500 吨/升/加仑。

234. I received/supplied aviation gasoline, quantity 2000 gallons. 我舰接收/供应航空汽油 2000 加仑（1 英加仑≈4.5464 升）。

235. Replenish/transfer potable water by close-in rig at station No. 03 from STBD side of me. 我舰右舷 3 号补给站用内牵索补给/传送饮用水。

236. Reduce speed to stream/recover astern fueling rig (to×× knots). 减速（到××节），投放/回收舰尾油料补给缆索。

237. Ready to commence disengagement. 准备好开始脱离。

238. By night the Morse equivalents of ROMEO and PREP may be flashed four times during replenishment operations, using the following colored lights as appropriate: WHITE Light Signal- at the DIP; RED Light Signal- CLOSE UP. 夜间补给时，可用以下灯光发送等同于 ROME 旗和 PREP 旗的摩尔斯码信号四次：白色灯光信号等同于升旗一半；红色灯光信号等同于升旗到杆顶。

239. Ships in replenishment units alter course as directed by their control ship (s) so as to preserve relative bearings and distances from their replenishment unit guide. 编入补给单位的舰艇根据其指挥舰的指令改变航向，以便与补给单位的引导舰保持相对方位和距离。

240. Ships not in replenishment units are to preserve true bearings and distances from the formation guide. 未编入补给单位的舰艇应与编队引导舰保持真方位和距离。

241. On receipt of the signal CORPEN N or SPEED L, ships replenishing alongside and/or astern report BF to the control ship when ready to commence the alteration. 接收到 CORPEN N(航向 N)或 SPEED L(航速 L)的信号后，正在进行横向补给或舰尾补给，或同时进行这两种作业的舰艇应向指挥舰发送 BF 报告，通报本舰已做好转向准备。

XI Port Call 舰艇出访

242. I'd like to discuss with you the visiting schedule of our task group. 我想与您讨论一下编队的访问计划。

243. Our task group will arrive at ××× harbor at 1100hrs, October the 20th, local time. 我们的编队将于当地时间 10 月 20 日 11 时抵达×××港。

244. How many ships are there in the task group? 编队中有多少艘舰艇？

245. Who is appointed to be the commander of the task group? 任命谁担任编队指挥员？

246. The command center/command post of the task group is stationed onboard DDG153. 编队指挥中心/指挥部设在 153 驱逐舰。

247. I will send all these data through fax/telex/telegram to my naval headquarters immediately. 我立即通过传真/电传/电报将这些数据上报给我们的海军司令部。

248. Proceed to weigh the anchors and cast off lines and set sail from the base. 开始起锚解缆，从基地出航。

249. Will the ××× Navy send any ships to meet us and escort us through the waterway into the port? ×××国海军是否将派遣舰艇与我会合，并护送我们通过水道进港？

250. We want to know the position of the rendezvous point (RV point), the time of rendezvous and the means of identification. 我们想知道会合点的位置、会合时间和识别方式。

251. The rendezvous point will be located somewhere about 17 nautical miles off the Signal Tower. 会合点定于距信号塔 17 海里处。

252. As for the means of identification, you can stand by at IMM (International Maritime Mobile Service) VHF Channel 13 and 16 by the time when you are about to arrive at the rendezvous point. 至于识别方式，贵国编队可以在即将到达会合点的时候在国际海上移动通信业务甚高频13频道和16频道收听。

253. ××× VTIS East Sector, ××× VTIS East Sector. This is Chinese naval ship CNS XI'AN calling. Can you hear me? Over. ×××国东区交通管制中心，×××国东区交通管制中心，中国海军舰艇"西安"号正在呼叫。能否听见？

254. Chinese naval ship, this is ××× VTIS. I read you loud and clear. Go ahead. Over. 中国海军舰艇，这里是×××国东区交通管制中心。你的通话响亮清晰。请继续。

255. Here is ××× VTIS East Sector. What is your name and call sign? 这里是×××国东区交通管制中心。你的舰名和呼号是什么？

256. XI'AN and GAO YOU HU, how to spell your names? Over. "西安"号和"高邮湖"号，怎样拼写你们的舰名？

257. Our names are X-ray India Alfa November for XI'AN. And the other ship's name is Golf Alfa Oscar Yankee Oscar Uniform Hotel Uniform for GAO YOU HU. Over. 我们的舰名是X-I-A-N，即"西安"号。另一艘舰的舰名是G-A-O-Y-O-U-H-U，即"高邮湖"号。

258. Roger. XI'AN and GAO YOU HU. Please inform your position. 明白。"西安"号和"高邮湖"号。请通报舰位。

259. My position is 5°32.4′N, 106°42′E. Over. 我舰位置在北纬5°32.4′，东经106°42′。

260. What is your ETA (Estimated Time of Arrival) to ××× lighthouse? Over. 预计何时抵×××灯塔？

261. Do you intend to enter harbor or transit the strait? 贵舰是打算进港还是通过海峡？

262. You are proceeding on a dangerous course. Alter course to 123 degrees. 你航向上有危险。转向至123°。

263. You may resume your previous course. 你可以恢复原来的航向。

264. You must change your course at once, or you will be in danger of striking a reef. 你必须立即改变航向，否则将有触礁的危险。

265. My full maneuvering speed is 24 knots. 我的操纵全速是 24 节。

266. Maximum speed in tow is 12 knots. 拖带时最大航速 12 节。

267. I can only proceed at slow speed. 我只能以低速前进。

268. I am increasing /reducing speed. 我正在加/减速。

269. My vessel is stopped and making no way through the water. 我舰已停车，对水速度为零。

270. How many revolutions does your propeller make at full speed? 你船全速时推进器转速多少？

271. My position is 9°36′N, 32°28′E. 我的位置是北纬 9°38′，东经 32°28′。

272. My position is ascertained by dead reckoning/visual bearings. 我的位置是推算/由目测方位确定的。

273. Close down radio watch on two-five-three decimal four Megahertz (or on VHF channel 69). 停止在 253.4 兆赫频率(甚高频 69 频道)上收听。

274. I am not in radio communication with you on 625 kilohertz. Check your transmitter (receiver). 我无法在 625 千赫频率上与你通信。检查你的发射机（接收机）。

275. Establish communications with me by flag hoist. 以升旗方式与我建立通信联系。

276. I wish to communicate with you by semaphore (telegraph system to covey message). 我想与你进行手旗通信。

277. Commence the signal exercise by flashing light (this is called flashing). 开始灯光信号演练。

278. The firing area is enclosed by the four coordinates: 24°21′N, 53°33′E; 24°37′N, 53°42′E; 24°40′N, 53°27′E; 24°47′N, 53°35′E. 射击海域由下列四个坐标围成：北纬 24°21′，东经 53°33′；北纬 24°37′，东经 53°42′；北纬 24°40′，东经 53°27′；北纬 24°47′，东经 53°35′。

279. Close to me on starboard side for transfer of fuel at forward transfer station. 从左舷靠近我舰在前方位进行油料输送。

280. I have mail/light material for light line (or life line) transfer on my starboard side. 我有邮件(轻装物资)在我右舷以轻质输送缆方式输送。

281. I require 600 US gallons of distillate fuel by probe coupling. 我需要以探针连接器方式加装 600 加仑(1 美加仑=3.785 升)馏出燃料。

282. I received/supplied 2000 liters of potable water. 我已加装/输送 2000 升饮用水。

283. Stream/recover fueling rig. 伸出/收回加油装置。

284. Duration of RAS is 40 minutes. 海上补给需时 40 分钟。

285. Do not proceed until I inform you. 等我通知后你再继续航行。

286. Please abide by the United Nations Convention on the Law of the Sea and the laws of the People's Republic of China. 请你遵守《联合国海洋法公约》和中华人民共和国法律。

287. You are exempted from pilot age. 你船免除引水。

288. Could you send us a pilot? 你能为我们派一名引水员吗?

289. At what position can I take the pilot? 我船在什么地方上引水员?

290. Should I rig pilot ladder or gangway? 我应安放引水梯, 还是舷梯?

291. Rig pilot ladder on port side 3 meters above water. 在左舷距水面 3 米处安放引水梯。

292. Man ropes are required. 需要扶手绳。

293. Embarkation is not possible due to the rough sea. 风浪太大, 不能登船。

294. Is pilotage compulsory? 引水是强制性的吗?

295. HMS ×××, HMS ×××. This is PLANS 572. Intention: I will overtake you on your port side. 某国海军"×××"号, 某国海军"×××"号。这是中国海军 572 舰。意图: 我将从你左舷追越。

296. PLANS 572, this is HMS ×××. Agree. Advice: keep sufficient lateral distance. 中国海军 572 舰, 这是某国海军"×××"号。同意追越。建议: 请保

持足够的横距。

297. I am approaching you on your port quarter. My present speed: 14 knots. 我正从你左舷舷尾接近。我舰当前航速 14 节。

298. Warning: I am steering at high speed. You are in danger of collision with me. 警告：我正高速航行。有碰撞危险。

299. Instruction: do not cross ahead of me. Advise you cross astern of me. 指示：不要从我舰前方通过。建议你舰从我舰后方通过。

300. Please keep to your starboard side of sea lane when we meet. I need sufficient space to clear obstructions. 会船时请保持在航道右侧航行。我需要足够的空间避开障碍物。

附录 3

海上联演英文缩略语和术语

缩略语/术语	英文全称	中文
A/R	As Required	按要求
AAA	Anti-Aircraft Artillery	高射炮
AAC	Airborne Aircraft Controller	飞行控制器
AADC	Area Air Defense Commander	区域防空指挥官
AADP	Area Air Defense Plan	区域防空计划
AALC	Amphibious Assault Landing Boat	两栖突击登陆艇
AAM	Air to Air Missile	空对空导弹
AAMEX	Air to Air Missile Exercise	空对空导弹演习
AAR	Air to Air Refueling/After Action Report	空中加油/行动后报告
AAV	Amphibious Assault Vehicle	两栖突击车
AAW	Anti-Air Warfare	防空战
AAWC	Anti-Air Warfare Commander	防空作战指挥官
ABBREV	Abbreviation	缩略语
ABN	Abnormal	异常
ABO	Assistant Boarding Officer	登临副指挥官
ACA	Air Control Authority/Airspace Control Authority	空中管理局/空域控制权
ACC	Attack Clearance Cell	攻击批准部位
ACC. L.	Accommodation Ladder	舷梯
ACE	Air Combat Element/Assistant Chief Engineer	空战单元/副机电长
ACFT	Aircraft	飞机
ACIXS	Allied Command Information Exchange System	联合指挥信息交换系统
ACOCC	Air Combat Operations Command Center	空战作战指挥中心
ACSA	Acquisition and Cross-Servicing Agreements	采购及交叉勤务协议
ACTS	Aegis Combat Training System	宙斯盾作战训练系统
ACU	Air/Aircraft Control Unit	空管单位
ACV	Air-Cushion Vehicle	气垫船
AD/WASEX	Air Defense/War at Sea Exercise	防空/海上作战演习
ADA	Air Defense Artillery	防空炮
ADC	Air Defense Commander	防空指挥官

续附表

缩略语/术语	英文全称	中文
ADC/R	Air Defense Command and Reporting	防空指挥与报告
ADFOR	Advanced Force	先遣部队
ADFT	Aft Draft	艉吃水
ADG	Degaussing Ship	消磁船
ADIZ	Air Defense Identification Zone	防空识别区
ADP	Air Defense Plan/Automated Data Processing	防空计划/自动数据处理
ADS	Air Defense Ship	防空舰
ADWC	Air Defense Warfare Commander	防空作战指挥官
ADZC	Amphibious Defense Zone Coordinator	两栖防空区协调官
AE	Ammunition Ship	弹药船
AEZ	Air Exclusion Zone	空中管制区
AF	Air Force/Audio Frequency/Store Ship	空军/声频/补给船；仓库船
AFB	Air Force Base	空军基地
AFS	Combat Store Ship	战斗补给舰
AFSB	Afloat Forward Staging Base	海上浮动前进码头或基地
AFT	—	船尾
AGL	Above Ground Level	超地平线
AGS	Surveying Ship	测量船
AH	Hospital Ship	医院船
AIC(S)	Air Intercept Controller (Supervisor)	空中拦截控制器(超级)
AIO	Action Information Organization	战斗/作战信息组织
AIRBORNE/OFF DECK	Airborne/Off Deck	起飞
A-J	Anti Jam	抗干扰/抗阻塞
ALCON	All Concerned	所有相关单位
ALRIMPAC	All Rim of the Pacific	所有环太平洋参演单位
ALT	Alternate	轮流
ALTREVS	Altitude Reservations	预留高度
AMID	Amidships	舰船中段
AMPN	Amplification/Amplifying Line in a Message/Signal	信息/信号放大线
AMRAAM	Advanced Medium-Range Air-to-Air Missile	高级中程空对空导弹

续附表

缩略语/术语	英文全称	中文
AMSL	Above Mean Sea Level	平均海平面上
AMW	Amphibious Warfare	两栖战
AMWC	Amphibious Warfare Commander	两栖战指挥官
AO	Action Officer/Area of Operations	作战行动军官/作业区
AOA	Amphibious Objective Area	两栖目标区
AOE	Fast Combat Support Ship	快速战斗支援舰
AOR	Area of Responsibility/Auxiliary Oiler Replenishment	任务区或责任区/辅助油料补给舰
AP	Transport/Antipersonnel	运输舰/反步兵
APAN	All Partners Access Network	参演方(所有伙伴国)接入网
APCSS	Asia-Pacific Center for Security Studies	亚太安全研究中心
ARG	Amphibious Ready Group	两栖战备大队
ARM	Armed Resistance Movement/Anti-Radiation Missile	武装抵制运动(武装集团)/反辐射导弹
ARR	Arrival	抵达
AS	Associated Support/Attack Skiff	联合支援/攻击性小艇
ASAC	Anti-Submarine Aircraft Controller	反潜飞机控制器
ASAP	As Soon As Possible	尽快
ASCM	Anti Ship Cruise Missile	反舰巡航导弹
ASL	Above Sea Level	海平面上
ASM	Air-to-Surface Missile/Anti-Ship Missile	反舰导弹
ASROC	Anti-Submarine Rocket	反潜火箭
ASST	Anti-Ship Surveillance & Targeting	反舰监视与瞄准
AST	Armed Security Team	武装安全小组
ASTAC	Anti-Submarine/Anti-Surface Tactical Air Controller	反潜/舰空中战术指挥官
ASUW	Anti-Surface Warfare	反舰战
ASW	Anti-Submarine Warfare	反潜战
ASWACU	Anti-Submarine Warfare Aircraft Control Unit	反潜战飞机控制单元
ASWC	Anti-Submarine Warfare Commander	反潜战指挥官
ASWEX	Anti-Submarine Warfare Exercise (Firing Event)	反潜演习(实弹射击项目)
ASWFA	Anti-Submarine Warfare Free Area	自由反潜区

续附表

缩略语/术语	英文全称	中文
ASWOC	Anti-Submarine Warfare Operations Center	反潜战作战中心
ASWS	Anti-Submarine Weapon System	反潜武器系统
ASWSOW	Anti-Submarine Warfare Stand-off Weapon	防区外发射的反潜武器
AT	Anti-Terrorism	反恐
ATAC	Advanced Torpedo Acoustic Control (System)	高级鱼雷声学控制(系统)
ATDS	Aircraft Tactical Data System	机载战术数据系统
ATF	Amphibious Task Force	两栖特混部队
ATG	Amphibious Task Group	两栖特混编队
ATSG	Aegis Training Support Group	宙斯盾训练支援大队
ATT	at this time	目前
ATW	Ahead Thrown Weapon System	火箭深弹武器系统
AWE	Advanced Warfighting Experiment	高级作战试验
AWEX	Air Warfare Exercise	空战演习
AWS	Aegis Weapon System	宙斯盾武器系统
AWWS	Above Water Weapons System	水面武器系统
B2B/BTB	Bridge to Bridge	驾驶室对驾驶室；舰桥对舰桥
BARRA	Type of Sonobuoy	超声波浮标类型
BB	Battleship/Breakbulk	战列舰/散装
BBS	Bulletin Board System	公告板系统
BCA	Broadcast Control Authority	广播控制局
BCO	Base Communications Office	基础通信办公室
BCST/BCAST	Broadcast	广播
BDA	Battle Damage Assessment	战损评估报告
BDR	Battle Damage Repair	战斗损害恢复
BF	Battle Force	战斗部队
BFM	Basic Fighter Manuevers	基础战斗机动
BFS	Beaufort Wind Scale	蒲福风级表
BGIT	Battle Group Integrated Training	战斗队整体训练
BGLC	Battle Group Logistics Commander	战斗队后勤指挥官
BIF	Bilateral Force	双边军事力量

续附表

缩略语/术语	英文全称	中文
BLK	Block	封锁
BLOS	Beyond the Line-of-Sight	超视距
BMP	Best Management Practice	最佳应对措施
BO	Boarding Officer	登临指挥官
BOWTS	Bigle and Oily Waste Treatment System	舱底废油水处理系统
BPSC	Bearing per Steering Course	舵罗经方位
BPT	Be Prepared to	准备……
BRF	Brief	简介
BSC/BSF/BSP	Brief Stop for Cargo/Brief Stop for Fuel/Brief Stop for Personnel	货物转载短暂停留/油料转运短暂停留/人员换乘短暂停留
BSR	Broadcast Screen Request	视屏广播申请
BT	Bathythermograph/Boarding Team/Break Transition	深海温度测量器/临检队/结束，转至
BTM	Boarding Teams	登临小组
BVP	Beacon Video Processor	信号浮标视频处理器
BVR	Beyond Visual Range	超视距
BWC	Battle Watch Captain	作战观察员
BWO	Battle Watch Officer	作战值更官
C&R	Circuit and Radio/Coordination and Reporting	通信网络/协调报告网络
C/C	Commander/Coordinator	指挥官/协调官
C/S	Call Sign	呼号
C^2	Command and Control	指挥与控制
C^3	Command, Control and Communications	指挥、控制与通信
C3F	Commander, 3rd Fleet	第3舰队司令
C^3I	Command, Control and Communications, and Intelligence	指挥、控制、通信与情报
C^4I	Command, Control, Communications, Computers and Intelligence	指挥、控制、通信、计算机与情报
C^4ISR	Command, Control, Communications, Computers, Intelligence, Surveillance, and Reconnaissance	指挥、控制、通信、计算机、情报、监视与侦察
CA	Combat Assessment/Heavy Cruiser	作战评估/重巡洋舰
CABL	Cable = One Tenth of one nautical mile (2000 yards)	链，10链=1海里（2000码）

续附表

缩略语/术语	英文全称	中文
CADS	Combined Air Defense System	联合防空系统
CAF	Commander Amphibious Force	两栖部队指挥官
CANTCO	Cannot Comply	无法答应
CAOC	Combined Air Operations Center	联合空战中心
CAS	Close Air Support/Collaboration at Sea	近距空中支援/海上协同
CASEVAC	Casualty Evacuation	伤员后撤
CASEX	Combined Anti-Submarine Warfare Exercise	联合反潜演习
CASREP	Casualty Report	伤员报告
CATAS	Critical Angle Towed Array System	临界角拖曳线列阵系统
CATCC	Carrier Air Traffic Control Center	航母空中交通管制中心
CATF	Commander Amphibious Task Force	两栖特混部队指挥官
CBMU	Construction Battalion Mobile Unit	建设营机动小队
CBR	Chemical Biological and Radiological	生化辐射
CBT	Computer-Based Training	计算机辅助训练
CCA	Carrier Controlled Approach/Carrier Controlled Area	航母受控接近/航母受控区
CCAO	Combined Crisis Action Organization	联合危机行动组织
CCCC	Combined Communication Control Center	联合通信控制中心
CCF3	Commander Escort Flotilla 3 (Comcortflot Three)	第3护航支队指挥官
CCIR	Critical Information Requirements	关键信息请求
CCO	Chief of Combat Operations	指挥作战长
CCOI	Critical Contact of Interest	高价值目标
CCS	Combined Control System/Communications Control Ship	集中控制系统/通信指挥舰
CCSG-9	Commander Carrier Strike Group-9	第9航母打击大队司令
CCSS	Cryptologic Combat Support System	加密作战支援系统
CCTF	Commander Combined Task Force	联合特混编队司令
CCWS	Cryptologic Combat Weapon System	加密作战武器系统
CDC	Combat Direction Center	作战指挥中心
CDCM	Coastal Defense Cruise Missiles	岸防巡航导弹
CDS-31	Commander Destroyer Squadron-31	第31驱逐舰中队指挥官
CECG	Combined Exercise Control Group	联合演习控制(导调)组

续附表

缩略语/术语	英文全称	中文
CENTRIXS	Combined Enterprise Regional Information Exchange System	联合力量地区信息共享系统
CEOD1	Commander Eod Group (Comeodgru) One	第1排爆大队司令
CERTSUB	Contact Positively Identified As a Submarine	主动识别潜艇
CEWN	Command Emergency Warning Net	紧急告警网
CEXC	Combined Explosives Exploitation Cell	联合爆炸物勘察小组
CFACC	Combined Force Air Component Commander	联合部队空中兵力指挥官
CFLCC	Combined Force Land Component Commander	联合部队地面部队指挥官
CFMCC	Combined Force Maritime Component Commander	联合部队海上兵力指挥官
CFOTC	Combined Force Over the Horizon Track Coordinator	联合部队超视距跟踪协调官
CFSOCC	Combined Forces Special Operations Component Command	联合部队特种作战兵力指挥官
CFST	Contaminated Fuel Settling Tank	受污燃油处理舱
CG	Guided Missile Cruiser	导弹巡洋舰
CGN	Nuclear Powered Guided Missile Cruiser	核动力导弹巡洋舰
CHL/CH	Channel	频道
CHOP	Change of Operational Control	作战指挥权转换
CHT	Collection, Holding and Transfer System	(污水)接纳转头系统
CI	Civilian Internees	被拘留的平民
CIB	Combined Information Bureau	联合信息中心
CIC	Combat Information Center	作战情报中心
CICC	Combat Information Center Commander	作战情报中心(舰艇作战室)指挥官
CIDC	Combat Identification Coordinator	作战识别协调官
CIP	Come in Please/Critical Infrastructure Protection	请讲/重要设施保护措施
CIS	Communications and Information Systems	通信和信息系统
CISE	Combined Intelligence Support Element	联合情报支援单元
CIWS	Close-in Weapon System	近程武器防御系统
CJA	Command Judge Advocate	指挥评判员
CJCS	Chairman of the Joint Chiefs of Staff	参谋长联席会主席
CJMD	Combined Joint Manning Document	联合人事档案
CJTF	Combined Joint Task Force	联合特遣部队

续附表

缩略语/术语	英文全称	中文
CLAN	Combined Local Area Network	联合局域网
CLF	Combat Logistic Force/Commander Land Force	作战后勤部队/地面部队指挥官
CLO	Combat Logistics Force Logistics Officer	作战后勤部队后勤官
CMA	Comma	逗号
CMCC	Civil-Military Coordination Center	军地协调中心
CMF	Combined Maritime Forces	多国海上力量
CMFU	Combined Metoc Forecast Unit	联合气象预报单元
CMIO	Communications Material Issuing Office	通信材料发布办公室
CMNT	Comment	评论
CMO	Civil Military Operations/Combined Metoc Officers	平民军事作战/联合气象官
CMOC	Civil-Military Operations Center	军民联合作战中心
CMSP	Commander Maritime Warfare Systems Pacific	太平洋海上作战系统指挥官
CNA	Center for Naval Analysis	海军分析中心
CND	Computer Network Defense	计算机网络防御
CNO	Chief of Naval Operations	海军作战部长
CNRH	Commander, Navy Region Hawaii	夏威夷地区海军司令
CNS	Chief of the Naval Staff	海军参谋长
CNX	Cancel	取消
CO	Commanding Officer	指挥官,舰长
COA	Combined Operating Area/Course of Action	联合作战区/行动方向
COAF	Coalition/Combined Operational Area Forecasts	联合作战区广播
COCOM	Combatant Command (Command Authority)	战斗指挥(指挥授权)
COD	Carrier Onboard Delivery	航母舰载补给
CODAG	Combined Diesel and Gas Turbine	柴油机与燃气轮机联合推进装置
CODAR	Correlations, Detection, Analysis and Recording System	关联、侦察、分析与记录系统
CODOG	Combined Diesel or Gas Turbine	柴油机与燃气轮机交替使用联合推进装置
COH	Cargo on Hand	现有货物
COI	Contact of Interest	嫌疑目标
COLREGS	Collision Regulations (International Regulations for Preventing Collision at Sea)	《国际海上避碰规则》

续附表

缩略语/术语	英文全称	中文
COMDESRON	Commander, Destroyer Squadron	驱逐舰中队指挥官
COMEX	Commence Exercise	开始演习
COMINT	Communications Intelligence	通信情报
COMMEX	Communication Exercise	通信演习
COMNAV	Commander Naval Aviation	海军航空兵司令
COMPACFLT	Command, Pacific Fleet	太平洋舰队司令部
COMPTUEX	Composite Training Unit Exercise	复合训练单元演习
COMSUBPAC	Command Submarine Pacific	太平洋潜艇司令部
COMTHIRDFLT	Command, Third Fleet	第3舰队司令部
COMWAR	Commanding Officer Maritime Warfare	海上战斗指挥官
CONOPS	Concept of Operations/Convoy Operations	行动方案/编队行动
CONPLAN	Concept of Operations Plan	作战计划概念
CONREP	Connected Replenishment	连续补给
COORD	Coordinated/Coordination/Coordinator	协同，协调官
COP	Common Operating White Shipping Picture	船舶信息图，通用作战图
COS	Chief of Staff	参谋长
CP	Counter Piracy	反海盗
CPA(TCPA)	(Time of) Closest Point of Approach	最近接近距离（时间）
CPI	Coastal Patrol and Interdiction	海岸巡逻和封锁
CPR7	Commander Amphibious Squadron Seven	第7两栖中队指挥官
CPX	Command Post Exercise	指挥所演习
CQ	Carrier Landing Qualifications	航母着降资格
CR	Close Range (Weapons Systems)	近程（武器防御系统）
CROE	Combined Rules of Engagement	联合交战规则
CRS	Coastal Riverine Squadron	海岸中队
CRTS	Casualty Receiving Treatment Ship	伤员接收治疗船
CRV	Combat Reconnaissance Vehicle	作战侦察车
CSAR	Combat Search and Rescue	作战搜救
CSARTF	Combat Search and Rescue Task Force	作战搜救部队
CSC	Combat System Coordinator	作战系统协调官
CSE	Course	航向

续附表

缩略语/术语	英文全称	中文
CSF	Carrier Strike Force	航母打击部队
CSFMP	Combat System Frequency Management Program	作战系统频谱管理计划
CSG	Carrier Strike Group	航母打击大队
CSO	Center of Special Operations/Chief Staff Officer	特战指挥中心/参谋长
CSOTF	Combined Special Operations Task Force	联合特种作战部队
CSP	Commander Submarine Forces Pacific (Comsubpac)	太平洋潜艇部队指挥官
CSRC	Combined Search and Rescue Cell	联合搜救单元
CSSD	Combat Services Support Detachment	作战服务支援分遣队
CSSE	Combat Services Support Element	作战支援单元
CSSG	Combat Services Support Group	作战支援大队
CSTOM	Combat Systems Technical Operations Manual	作战系统技术作战手册
CSV	Counter Surveillance	反跟踪
CSW	Crew-Served Weapons	轻武器
CT	Computed Tomography	计算机断层扫描
CTAPS	Contingency Theater Automated Planning System	战区偶然事件自动计划系统
CTF	Commander Task Force/Combined Task Force	特混舰队指挥官/联合特混编队
CTG	Combined Task Group	联合特混大队
CTP	Common Tactical Picture	通用战术图像
CTTG	Counter-Targeting	反瞄准
CTU	Combined/Commander Task Unit	特混小队/小队指挥官
CU	Common Unit	通用单元
CUDIXS	Common User Digital Information Exchange System	通用数据信息交换系统
CUES	Code for Unplanned Encounters at Sea	《海上意外相遇规则》
CV	Aircraft Carrier (Non Nuclear Powered)	航空母舰(无核动力)
CVBG	Carrier Battle Group	航母战斗大队
CVIC	Carrier Intelligence Center	航母情报中心
CVN	Nuclear Powered Aircraft Carrier	核动力航空母舰
CVOA	Carrier Operating Area	航母作战区
CVTG	Carrier Task Group	航母特混大队
CVW-2	Carrier Fixed Wing-2	航母固定翼联队-2
CW	Clockwise	顺时针方向

续附表

缩略语/术语	英文全称	中文
CWC	Combined Warfare Command	联合作战指挥
CZ	Control Zone	控制区域
D/CCTF	Deputy Commander Combined Task Force	联合特混部队副指挥
DA	Defended Area/Direct Action/Distribution Authority	防卫区/直接行动/分配授权
DAL	Defended Asset List	有利防御列表
DAR	Designated Areas of Recovery	指定恢复区
DARPA	Defense Advanced Research Project Agency	高级防御研究项目代理
DART	Disaster Assistance Response Team	救灾反应队
DCA	Defensive Counter Air	防御性对空行动
DCAM	Defense Counter Air Mission	防御防空任务
DCAST	Data Collection and Scheduling Tool	数据收集与计划工具
DCMS	Director, Communication Security Material System	通信安全物质系统主任
DCO	Depth Cut Out	深度裁剪
DCU	Defense Communications Unit	防御通信单元
DD	Destroyer	驱逐舰
DDG	Guided Missile Destroyer	导弹驱逐舰
DDN	Nuclear Powered Destroyer	核动力驱逐舰
DE	Damage Expectancy	损伤评估
DEP	Departure	离港
DESIGN	Designation	指定
DESRON	Destroyer Squadron	驱逐舰中队
DESTIN	Destination	目的地,目的港
DET	Detachment	分队
DF	Detection Finding	测向
DIMS	Daily Intention Messages	演习计划日报
DISUM	Daily Intelligence Summary	每日情报总结
DIVTACS	Division Tactics	分队战术机动
DIW	Dead in Warfare/Dead in Water	战斗牺牲/停车状态
DLI	Deck Launched Interceptor	舰载拦截机
DMA	Dangerous Military Activity	危险军事活动
DMZ	Demilitarized Zone	非军事区

续附表

缩略语/术语	英文全称	中文
DOB	Depth of Burst	爆炸深度
DOD	Department of Defense	[美]国防部
DOIC	Deputy Officer in Charge	副指挥员
DOS	Department of State	[美]国务院
DRACO	Disputant Resistance Armed Combatant Opposition	反对派武装力量
DRESS	—	降落
DSC	Disress Call	求救信号
DSCS	Defense Satellite Communications System	国防卫星通信系统
DSN	Defense Switched Network	国防交换网络
DSV	Deep Submergence Vehicle	深潜潜水器
DTG	Date Time Group	日期时间组码(日期、时间、批号)
DTMF	Dual Tone Multi-Frequency	双音多频
DTS	Direct Transmission/Data Terminal Set	直接传送/数据终端集合
DWT	Dead Weight	载重吨位
E/E	Entry/Exit (Point)	进口/出口(点)
EA	Electronic Attack	电子攻击
EBE	Event-By-Event	项目接项目
ECCM	Electronic Counter-Counter Measures	电子反对抗
ECM	Electronic Counter Measure	电子对抗
EDATF	Emergency Defense Amphibious Task Force	两栖特混部队紧急事件防御
EE	Environment and Energy	环境与能源
EEZ	Exclusive Economic Zone	专属经济区
EFIS	Electronic Flight Information System	电子飞行信息系统
EHF	Extremely High Frequency	极高频
EIA	Enlisted Intelligence Assistant	现役情报助手
EID	Electronic Identification	电子识别
ELF	Extremely Low Frequency	极低频
ELINT	Electronic Intelligence/Electromagnetic Intelligence	电子情报/电磁情报
ELSW	Elsewhere	别处,其他地方
EM	Explosive Material	爆炸物
EMATT	Expendable Mobile Anti-Submarine Warfare Target	消耗性移动反潜目标

续附表

缩略语/术语	英文全称	中文
EMC	Electromagnetic Compatibility	电磁兼容
EMI	Electromagnetic Interference	电磁干扰
EMO	Enhanced Marine Air Ground Task Force Operations	联合海陆空特混作战
EMP	Electromagnetic Pulse	电磁脉冲
ENE	East-North-East	东北东
ENG	Engineering	主机
ENR	En Route	航渡中
EOD	Explosive Ordnance Disposal	爆炸物处理
EODMU	Explosive Ordance Disposal Mobile Unit	排爆机动小队
EOM	End of Message	消息结束
EOT	Engine Order Telegraph	机舱传令钟，机舱车钟
EPA	Evasion Plan of Action	行动后退计划
EPIRB	Emergency Position Indicating Radio Beacon	紧急无线电定位标
EPLRS	Enhanced Position Location Reporting System	加强版定位报告系统
ES	Electronic Support	电子支援
ESC	Electronics Systems Center/Escort	电子信息中心/护航
ESG	Expeditionary Strike Group	远征打击大队
ESG SCC	Expeditionary Strike Group Sea Combat Commander	远征打击大队海上战斗司令部
ESM	Electronic Support Measures	电子支援措施
ESOC	Emergency Support Operations Center	紧急事故支援作战中心
ESSM	Evolved Sea Sparrow Missile	改进型海麻雀导弹
ETA	Estimated Time of Arrival	预计到达时间
ETB	Estimated Time of Berthing	预计靠泊时间
ETD	Estimated Time of Departure	预计离港时间
ETL	Earliest Time to Launch	最早时间发射
ETR	Estimated Time of Repair/Estimated Time Remaining	预计修复时间/预计剩余时间
ETS	Estimated Time of Sailing	预计起航时间
EW	Electronic Warfare	电子战
EWX	Electronic Warfare Exercise	电子战演习
EXCON	Exercise Control（Officer）	演习控制(官)

续附表

缩略语/术语	英文全称	中文
EXCOR	Exercise Coordinator	演习协调官
EXER	Exercise	演习，演练
EXINST	Exercise Instructions	演习指导
EXORD	Execute Order/Exercise Order	执行命令/演习指令
EXREADCON	Exercise Readiness Condition	演习备便条件
EXROE	Exercise Rules of Engagement	演习交战规则
EXROEAUTH	Exercise Rules of Engagement Authorised	演习交战规则授权
EXROECNX	Exercise Rules of Engagement Cancel	演习交战规则取消
EXROESUM	Exercise Rules of Engagement Summary	演习交战规则总结
EXTAC	Exercise Tactics	演习战术
EXTOR	Exercise Torpedoes	鱼雷演练
FA	Friendly Approach	友好接近，善意接近
FAA	Federal Aviation Administration/Fleet Air Arm	联邦航空行政中心/空中武器舰队
FAB	Frequency Availability Broadcast	有效频率广播
FAC	Fast Attack Craft/Forward Air Controller	快速攻击艇/前进气控制器
FAD	Fleet Air Defense	舰队空防
FADIZ	Fleet Air Defense Identification Zone	舰队空中防御识别区
FAM	Familiarization	熟悉
FAQ	Frequently-Asked Questions	常见问题
FAR	Federal Aviation Regulations	联邦航空规则
FARP	Forward Arming and Refueling Point	前武器与加油点
FAWC	Force Air Warfare Coordinator	空战协调官
FBL	Fly-By-Light	光传操纵系统
FBRD	Freeboard	干舷
FC	Fire Control	火控
FCC	Fleet Command Center	舰队指挥中心
FCF	Functional Check Flight	功能检查飞行
FCO	Fire Control Officer	灭火指挥官
FCS	Fire Control System	灭火系统
FCTC	Fleet Combat Training Center	舰队作战训练中心
FDFT	Fore Draft	艏吃水

续附表

缩略语/术语	英文全称	中文
FDO	Foreign Disclosure Officer	对外发布官
FDU	Fleet Diving Unit	舰队潜水分队
FEA	Fuel Exchange Agreements	油料交换协定
FEZ	Fighter Engagement Zone	交战区
FF	Frigate	护卫舰
FFG	Guided Missile Frigate	导弹护卫舰
FFIR	Friendly Force Intelligence Requirements	友邻部队情报需求
FFT	For Further Transfer/Friendly Force Tracking	待转派/友军位置跟踪
FFV	Fresh Fruits and Vegetables	新鲜水果和蔬菜
FHA	Foreign Humanitarian Assistance	外国人道主义救援
FHTNC	Fleet Hometown News Center	舰队家乡信息中心
FIAC	Fast Inshore Attack Craft	快速岸基攻击船
FIDC	Force Identification Coordinator	兵力识别协调官
FINEX	Finish Exercise	演习结束（时间）
FIP	Force Integretation Phase	兵力整合阶段
FISH	Fishing Vessels	渔船
FIT	Force Integration Training	兵力整合训练
FIWC	Fleet Information Warfare Center	舰队信息战中心
FL	Flight Level	飞行水平
FLC	Fleet Logistic Center	舰队后勤中心
FLCPH	Fleet Logistics Center Pearl Harbor	珍珠港舰队后勤中心
FLEACTS	Fleet Activities	舰队活动
FLETRAGRU	Fleet Training Group	舰队训练大队
FLEX	Fleet Experimentation	舰队实验
FLIP	Flight Information Publication	飞行信息出版物
FLI(s)	Forward Looking Infrared(System)	前置红外（系统）
FLS	Forward Logistics Site	前置后勤补给点
FLSS	Forward Logistics Support Site	前置后勤支援点
FLT	Flight	飞行
FLTCIC	Fleet Commander-In Chief	舰队总指挥
FLTTAC	Fleet Tactic	舰队战术信号

续附表

缩略语/术语	英文全称	中文
FLYPRO	Flying Program	飞行计划
FMC	Full Mission Capability	完全具备任务能力
FMF	Fleet Marine Force	舰队海上力量
FMPAC	Fleet Maritime Patrol Mobile Operations Control Center	舰队海上巡逻机动作战控制中心
FN	French Navy	法国海军
FNS	Foreign Nation Support/French Navy Ship	对外援助/法国海军舰艇
FOL	Follow	跟随
FOV	Field-of-View	视界
FP	Force Protection	兵力保护
FPC	Federal Power Commission/Final Planning Conference	联邦动力委员会/末期计划会
FPT	Full Period Termination	全周期终止
FR	Final Report	最终报告
FRAGO	Fragmentary Order	传送的补充命令
FRAM	Fleet Rehabilitation and Modernization	舰队重建与现代化建设
FREQS	Frequencies	频率
FSA	Fire Support Area/Fuel Support Agreement	火力支援区/能源服务协议
FSB	Fleet Satellite Broadcast	舰队卫星广播
FSCC	Fire Support Coordination Center	火力支援协调中心
FSO	Food Services Officer	食品供应军官
FST	Fleet Support Team/Fleet Surgical Team/Frequency Shift Telegraphy	舰队支援分队/舰队医疗分队/移频电报
FT	Feet	英尺
FTC	Force Track Coordinator	兵力跟踪协调官
FTI	Fixed Tactical Internet	固定战术网
FTOC	Fleet Telecommunications Operating Center	舰队电子通信作战中心
FTU	Fleet Training Unit	舰队训练单元
FTX	Field Training Exercise	战场训练演习
FUEL BARGE	—	燃油驳船
FVCR	Foreign Visit Clearance Request	外国访问通行证的请求
FVR	Foreign Visit Request	外交访问申请

续附表

缩略语/术语	英文全称	中文
FW	Fighter Wing/Fixed Wing	战机联队/固定翼
FWD	Forward	舰首方向，舰首
FYIP	For Your Information Please	供您参考
GALE	Generic Area Limitation Environment	一类环境限制保护区
GARS	Global Area Reference System	全球区域参考系统
GASS	Gyro Angled Snake Search	回转角式蛇形搜索
GAT	Guidance Apportionment and Targeting	引导指示和分配
GBU	Guided Bomb Units	引导炸弹单元
GCCS	Global Command and Control System/Global Command Communication System	全球指挥与控制系统/全球指挥通信系统
GCSB	Government Communications Security Bureau	政府通信安全局
GDSC	Global Distance Support Center	全球远距离支援中心
GENADMIN	General Administrative	总指挥
GENTEXT	General Text	总体信息
GLS	Global Logistics Support	全球后勤支援
GMDSS	Global Maritime Distress and Safety System	全球海上遇险与安全系统
GOP	General Operational Plot	全面作战标图
GOPO	Gas & Oil Platform Operations	油气作业平台
GPDC	General Purpose Digital Computer	普通目标数字电脑
GPHE	General Purpose High Effect (Bomb)	普通目标高能炸弹
GPS	Global Positioning System	全球定位系统
GSM	Global System for Mobile Communication	全球移动通信系统
GUNEX	Gunnery Exercise	舰炮射击演习
H/O	Hand Over	交接(重在交)
HA/DR	Humanitarian Affairs/Disaster Relief	人道主义事物/减灾
HAC	Helicopter Approach Controller	直升机接近控制官
HADR	Humanitarian Assistance and Disaster Relief	人道主义救援与减灾
HAILEX	Hail Exercise	通信演习
HAR	Helicopter Aerial Refueling	直升机空中加油

续附表

缩略语/术语	英文全称	中文
HATS	Hover Attack Torpedo System	旋回鱼雷攻击系统
HAZMAT	Hazardous Material	危险物资
HAZWASTE	Hazardous Waste	有害废物
HBROC/SLOC	Habor/Sea Lanes of Communication	港岸/海上交通线
HCS	Helicopter Control Ship/Helicopter Control Squadron	直升机母舰/直升机管理中队
HCSS	Helicopter Combat Support Squadron	直升机战斗支援中队
HCT	Helicopter Controller (Transit)	直升机管理运输
HD	High Drag (Bomb)	高空轰炸
HDC	Helicopter Direction Center	直升机引导中心
HDD	Head-Down Display	俯视显示仪
HDG	Heading	舰首
HDWS	High Definition Warning Surface (Radar)	高分辨率对海预警雷达
HEC	Helicopter Element Coordinator	直升机分队协调官
HEFOE	Hydraulics, Electric, Fuel, Oil, Engine (Code)	液压，电力，燃油，油料，主机(密码)
Heli-CASEVAC	Helicopter-Casualty Evacuation	直升机转运伤病员
HELO	Helicopter	直升机
HEPP	Heavy Equipment Purchase Program	重装备采购项目
HF	High Frequency	高频
HG/TG	Harpoon Grid/Talcon Grid	法军及中方用于固定直升机的钢网
HI	Hawaii/High	夏威夷/高
HIANG	Hawaii Air National Guard	夏威夷国民警卫队空军
HIFR	Helicopter In-Flight Refueling	直升机悬停加油
HIMEZ	High Missile Engagement Zone	高程导弹交战区
HIV	High Interest Vessel	高价值船舶
HIVL	High Interest Vessel List	高价值船舶列表
HM	Hazardous Material/Helicopter Mine Countermeasures Squadron	危险物品/直升机反水雷中队
HMAN	Her Majesty's Australian Navy	澳大利亚皇家海军
HMCN	Her Majesty's Canadian Navy	加拿大皇家海军
HMD	Helmet Mounted Display	头盔显示仪

续附表

缩略语/术语	英文全称	中文
HMMC	Hazardous Material Minimization Center	减少有害物中心
HMNZN	Her Majesty's New Zealand Navy	新西兰皇家海军
HMNZS	Her Majesty's New Zealand Ship	新西兰皇家海军舰艇
HMS	Helmet Mounted Sights/Her Majesty's Ship	头盔瞄准器/英国皇家海军舰艇
HN	Host Nation	主办国
HNS	Host Nation Support	东道国保障
HOA	Hawaiian Oparea	夏威夷作战区
HONEYPOT	Shipborne Beacon for Anti-Submarine Warfare Aircraft	反潜飞机的舰载指示灯
HP	Horse Power	马力
HRB	Horizontal Reference Bar	舰艇横摇指示器
HRS	Hours	时刻
HS	Helicopter Anti-Submarine Warfare Squadron/Helicopter Support Squadron	直升机反潜战中队/直升机支援中队
HSARM	High Speed Anti-Radiation Missile	高速反辐射导弹
HSC	Helicopter Support Coordinator	直升机支援协调官
HSCS	Helicopter Sub-Control Ship	直升机备降舰
HSL	Helicopter Anti-Submarine Warfare Squadron Light	轻型反潜直升机中队
HSMTS	High Speed Maneuverable Target System	海上高速机动拖靶系统
HSS	Health Service Support	公共医疗服务保障
HSTT	Hawaii Southern California Training and Testing	夏威夷南加利福尼亚训练和检测中心
HTC	Helicopter Transit Controller	直升机传递控制
HUD	Head-Up Display	平视显示仪
HVA	High Value Assets	高价值资产
HVU	High Value Unit/Hijacked Vessel Unit	高价值单元/扮演被劫船只
Hz	Hertz	赫兹
I&E	Intercept and Escort	拦截与护航
I&W	Indications and Warnings	指示与告警
IA	Implementing Arrangement	实施安排
IACS	Integrated Acoustic Communications System	综合声通信系统

续附表

缩略语/术语	英文全称	中文
IAD	International Air Distress	国际空难
IADS	Integrated Air Defence System	综合防空系统
IAEA	International Atomic Energy Agency	国际原子能机构
IAMSAR	International Aeronautical and Maritime Search and Rescue	国际航空和海上搜救手册
IAW	In Accordance With	与……一致,依照,根据
IBW	Information-Based Warfare	基于信息的战争
IC	Incident Commander	应急指挥官
ICAO	International Civil Aviation Organization	国际民航组织
ICC	International Chamber of Commerce	国际商会
ICD	Imitative Communications Deception	模仿通信欺骗
ICM	Intercommunication	内部通信系统,对讲机
ICN	Interface Coordination Net	接口协调网
ICO	Interface Control Officer	接口控制官
ICR	Initial Contact Reports	初联报告
ICS	Interphone Control System	内部通信控制系统
ICS/INTERCO	International Code of Signs	国际信号规则
ICT	Information Communication Technology	信息通信技术
ICU	Interface Control Unit/Intensive Care Unit	接口控制单元/重症监护室
ID	Identify, Identification	识别,身份证明
ID SUP/IDS	ID Supervisor/Identification Supervisor	证件检查员
IDD	International Direct Dial	国际直拨
IDLH	Immediately Dangerous to Life of Health	直接危害生命与健康
IDZ	Inner Defense Zone	内部防御区
IED	Improvised Explosive Device	简易爆炸装置
IEDD	Improvised Explosive Device Defeat/Inductance Energy Decay Device	反爆炸物/自制炸弹
IER	Information Exchange Region	信息交换区
IET	Intelligence Exploitation Team	情报获取分队
IFF	Identification Friend and Foe	敌我识别
IFR	In-Flight Refueling/Instrument Flying Rules	空中加油/飞行仪器规则
IFS	Integrated Food Services	综合食品服务

续附表

缩略语/术语	英文全称	中文
IIR	Imaging Infrared	红外成像
IMB	International Maritime Bureau	国际海事局
IMC	Instrument Meteorological Condition	专业仪器测量的气象条件
IMMS	International Maritime Mobile Service	国际海上移动通信业务
IMO	International Maritime Organization	国际海事组织
INCSEA	Incidents at Sea	海上意外
INFO	Information	信息
INFOTAC	Information Attack (Anti-Submarine Warfare Attack Made Using Third Party Target Position)	信息战（用第三方目标点反潜攻击）
INMARSAT	International Maritime Satellite	国际海事卫星
INOP	Inoperable	无法实行的
INS	Inertial Navigation System	惯性导航系统
INT	Interdiction/International	封锁/国际
INTEL	Intelligence	情报
INTREPS	Intelligence Reports	情报报告
IO	Information Operations/Intelligence Officer	信息作战/情报官
IOC	Initial Operational Capability/International Oceanographic Commission	初始作战能力/国际海洋学委员会
IOS	International Organization for Standardization	国际标准化组织
IOT	In Order to/Information Operation Team	为了，便于/信息情报分队
IPB	Intelligence Preparation of Battlespace	战斗区域情报准备
IR	Infrared	红外线
IRCR	International Committee of the Red Cross/Crescent	红十字会国际委员会
IRCS	International Radio Call Sign	国际无线电呼号
IRDS	Infrared Detection System	红外探测系统
IRLS	Infrared Line Scan	红外线扫描
IRST	Infrared Search and Track	红外搜索与跟踪
IS	Intelligence Specialist	情报专家
ISAR	Inverse Synthetic Aperture Radar	逆合成孔径雷达
ISD	Initial Search Depth	首发搜索深度
ISI	Initial Safety Inspection(=Clear)	安全
ISIC	Immediate Superior in Command	应急控制机构

续附表

缩略语/术语	英文全称	中文
ISO	In Support of/Information Security Officer/Instead of/International Science Organization/International Standards Organization	结合/信息安全官/代替/国际科学组织/国际标准化组织
ISR	Identification Safety Range/Intelligence, Surveillance and Reconnaissance	识别安全范围/情报、监视和侦察
ISSM	Information Systems Security Manager	信息系统安全管理
ITT	International Telephone and Telegraph Corporation	国际电话电报公司
ITU	International Telecommunication Union	国际电信联盟
IUSS	Integrated Undersea Surveillance System	综合水下监视系统
IVO	in the vicinity of	在……附近
IW	information warfare	信息战
IW-A	information attack	信息攻击
IW-D	information defend	信息保护
JAA	Joint Action Area	联合行动区
JAAT	Joint Aerial Attack Team	联合空中攻击小组
JAAWSC	Joint Anti-Air Warfare Shore Coordination (Net)	联合防空战港岸协调(网)
JAC	Joint Analysis Center	联合分析中心
JACOBS	Jacob's Ladder	软梯
JADO	Joint Air Defense Operations	联合防御作战
JADOCS	Joint Automated Deep Operations Coordinate System	联合自动深度作战协调系统
JAG	Judge Advocate General	总军法官
JAOC	Joint Air Operations Center	联合空战中心
JCS	Joint Chiefs of Staff	参谋长联席会议
JDISS	Joint Deployable Intelligence Support System	联合配置情报支援系统
JEZ	Joint Engagement Zone	联合交战区
JEZCU	Joint Engagement Zone Control Unit	联合作战区域控制单元
JFACC	Joint Force Air Component Commander	联合部队空中力量指挥官
JFC	Joint Force Commander	联合部队指挥官
JFLCC	Joint Force Land Component Commander	联合部队陆上力量指挥官
JFMCC	Joint Force Maritime Component Commander	联合部队海上力量指挥官
JIC	Joint Intelligence Center	联合情报中心
JICPAC	Joint Intelligence Center, Pacific	太平洋联合情报中心

续附表

缩略语/术语	英文全称	中文
JLC	Joint Logistics Center	联合后勤中心
JMAS	Joint Manning, Accommodation and Security	联合操控、调节和安全
JMCIS	Joint Maritime Command Information System	联合海上指挥信息系统
JMETS	Joint Mission Essential Tasks	联合需求任务
JMSDF	Japan Maritime Self Defense Force	日本海上自卫队
JOA	Joint Operating Area	联合作战区域
JOC	Joint Operations Center	联合作战中心
JOC BWO	Joint Operation Center Battle Watch Officer	联指作战值班员
JOPES	Joint Operational Planning and Execution System	联合作战计划与执行系统
JOTS	Joint Operations Tactical System	联合作战战术系统
JPAS	Joint Personnel Adjudication System	联合人事裁决系统
JPG	Joint Planning Group	联合计划组
JPR	Joint Personnel Recovery	联合人事恢复
JRC	Joint Reception Center	联合接收中心
JRCC	Joint Rescue Coordination Center	联合救援协调中心
JSOA	Joint Special Operations Area	联合专用作战区
JSOTF	Joint Special Operation Task Force	联合专项任务特混部队
JSRC	Joint Search and Rescue Center	联合搜救中心
JTAA	Joint Tactical Action Area	联合战术行动区
JTAC	Joint Tactical Air Controller	联合战术对空指挥员
JTAO	Joint Tactical Air Operations	联合战术空战
JTC	Joint Targeting Cell	联合瞄准单元
JTCB	Joint Target Coordination Board	联合瞄准协调板
JTF	Joint Task Force	联合特混编队
JTFEX	Joint Task Force Exercise	联合特混舰队演习
JTIDS	Joint Tactical Information Distribution System (Link 16)	联合战术信息分发系统(链16)
JTL	Joint Target List	联合目标列表
JU	Joint Unit	联合单元
KT/KTS	Knot/Knots	节
LARC	Light Amphicious Resupply Craft	轻型两栖补给艇
LAT/LONG	Latitude/Longitude	经纬度

续附表

缩略语/术语	英文全称	中文
LB/HP	Pound/Horse Power	磅/马力
LC	Landing Craft	登陆艇
LCA	Landing Craft, Assault	突击登陆艇
LCAC	Landing Craft, Air Cushion	气垫登陆艇
LCB	Logistics Coordination Board	后勤协调会
LCC	Logistics Coordination Centre/Amphibious Command Ship	后勤协调中心/两栖指挥舰
LCE	Logistics Combat Element	后勤作战单元
LCM	Landing Craft, Medium	中型登陆艇
LCP/LCL	Landing Craft, Personnel/Logistic	人员/后勤登陆艇
LCU	Landing Craft, Utility	效用登陆艇
LFX	Live Fire Exercises	实弹射击演习
LGB	Laser Guided Bomb	激光引导炸弹
LGP	Laser Guided Projectile	激光引导炮弹
LHA	Landing Helicopter Assault Ship/Amphibious Assault Ship	突击登陆直升机母舰/两栖通用攻击舰
LHD	Landing Helicopter Deck/Amphibious Assault Ship(Multipurpose)	船坞登陆直升机母舰/船坞两栖攻击舰
LL FREQUENCY	Landing/Launch Frequency	着舰/起飞频率
LMEZ	Low Missile Engagement Zone	低空导弹交战区
LNO/LO	Liason Officer	联络官
LOC	Logistic Operations Center	后勤业务中心
LOG	Logistic	后勤
LOG RUN	Logistics Run	后勤物资运送
LOGREQ	Logistic Request	后勤需求表
LOGSUMS	Logistic Summarys	后勤总结
LOI	Letter of Instruction	指导书
LOOS	Lines of Operations	作战区
LOP	Local Operational Plot	局部作战标图
Loran NAV	Long-Range Navigation	"罗兰"导航系统
LOS	Line of Sight/Law of the Sea	视距线/海洋法
LPH	Amphibious Assault Ship(Helicopter)	直升机两栖攻击舰
LPOC	Last Port of Call	上一港口
LRI	Low Risk of Intercept	低风险拦截

续附表

缩略语/术语	英文全称	中文
LRS	Logistics Readiness Squadron/Long Range Sonar	后勤战备中队/远距探测声呐
LSC	Logistics Support Center	后勤支援中心
LSD	Landing Ship, Dock	船坞登陆舰
LSE	Landing Safety Enlisted	降落安全引导员
LSF	Low Slow Flyer	低空慢速航空器
LSG	Logistics Support Group	后勤保障组
LSO	Landing Safety Officer/Logistics Support Officer	着舰安全引导官/后勤支援官
LSR	Logistics Support Representative	后勤支援代表
LSSS	Logistical Support, Supplies, and Services	后勤保障、物资和服务
LST	Landing Ship, Tank	坦克登陆舰
LSV	Logistic Support Vessel	后勤支援舰
LTL	Latest Time to Launch	最迟发射时间
LTRS	Letters	信件
LWT	Light Weight Torpedo	轻型鱼雷
M/V	Merchant Vessel	商船
MAB	Medical Air Bridge/Military Assault Boat	医疗空中桥梁/攻击快艇
MAD	Military Air Distress	军事空难
MAG	Maritime Action Group	海上行动大队
MAGTF	Marine Air Ground Task Force	海陆空特混编队
MALS	Marine Aircraft Logistics Squadron	海空后勤中队
MANPADS	Man Portable Air Defense System(s)	人工便携式防空系统
MARFOR	Marine Force	海上兵力
MARFORPAC	Marine Force Pacific	太平洋海上兵力
MARG	Marine Amphibious Ready Group	海上两栖备便大队
MARINTSUMS	Maritime Intelligence Summarys	海上情报总结
MARPAT	Maritime Patrol	海上巡逻
MARS	Military Affiliate Radio System	军联无线电系统
MASS CAS OPS	Mass Casualty Transfer Operations	大规模伤员后送
MATC	Medium-range Anti-Submarine Torpedo Carrying	中距反潜鱼雷运送
MATCONOFF	Material Control Officer	材料控制官
MAU	Maximum All Up (Weight)	最大载重
MAW	Marine Aircraft Wing	海空联队
MAX	Maximum	最大

续附表

缩略语/术语	英文全称	中文
MB	Marker Beacon/Motor Boat/Millibar	记号灯塔/摩托艇，快艇/毫巴
MBT	Main Battle Tank	主战坦克
MBU	Main Body Unit	主体单元
MC	Maneuvering Coordinator/Mission Coordinator	机动协调官/任务协调官
MCACCS	Marine Corps Air Command and Control System	陆战队空中指挥与控制系统
MCAF	Marine Corps Air Facility	陆战队空中设备
MCAR	Multi-Channel Acoustic Relay	多通道声学中继
MCBH	Marine Corps Base Hawaii	夏威夷陆战队基地
MCC	Maritime Command Center	海事指控中心
MCD	Mobile Communications Detachment	机动通信分遣队
MCM	Mine Counter Measures/Multi Command Manual	反水雷战，水雷对抗/多功能指挥手册
MCMC	Mine Counter Measures Coordinator	反水雷协调官
MCMEX	Mine Counter Measures Exercise	反水雷演习
MCMTA	Mine Counter Measures Tasking Authority/Task Administration	反水雷任务指挥部
MCMV	Mine Counter Measures Vessel	反水雷舰艇
MCOIN	Maritime Command Operations Information Network	海上指挥作战信息网
MCP	Mini Container Pool	支线船
MCS	Mine Countermeasure Ship	反水雷舰艇
MDA	Mine Danger Area	危险雷区
MDC	Mine Destruction Charge	灭雷弹；水雷摧毁装药
MDO	Marine Diesel Oil	航海柴油
MDSU	Mobile Diving and Savage Unit	机动潜水打捞小队
MDT	Maritime Dynamic Targeting	海上动态目标获取
MDV	Mine Disposal Vehicle	水雷处置船
MEA	Minimum En Route Safety Altitude	最小飞行安全高度
MEB	Marine Expeditionary Brigade	陆战队远征旅
MEDEVAC/CASEVAC	Medical Evacuation/Casualty Evacuation	医疗撤运/医疗后送
MEF	Marine Expeditionary Force	陆战队远征部队
MEG	Marine Expeditionary Group	陆战队远征大队
MERSHIPS	Merchant Ships	商船

续附表

缩略语/术语	英文全称	中文
MET	Mobile Environmental Team	机动环境小组
METOC	Meteorology and Oceanography/Meteorological and Oceanographic	气象与海洋学/气象与海洋学的
MEU	Marine Expeditionary Unit/Mission Essential Unit	陆战队远征小队/任务需求单元
MEZ	Missile Engagement Zone	导弹交战区
MF	Medium Frequency	中频
MFAS	Mid-Frequency Active Sonar	中频主动声呐
MFD	Medium False and Decline(Decay)/Main Multi-Function Display	中度故障或衰减/多功能主显示器
MFL	Multi-Frequency Link/Maritime Force Locator	多频率连接/海上兵力定位
MFP	Missing From Pier	从码头消失
MGO	Marine Gasolion Oil	海油
MHE	Material Handling Equipment	物资装卸设备
MHZ	Megahertz	兆赫
MI	Maritime Inspection/Mutual Interference	海上检查/相互干扰
MI & ISR	Maritime Interdiction & Intel Surveillance Recon	海上封锁与情报、监视和侦察
MIA	Missing in Action	行动中失踪
MID	Middle	中间
MIDPAC	Middle Pacific	中太平洋
MIF	Maritime Interception Force	海上拦截部队
MIJI	Meaconing, Interference, Jamming & Intrusion	虚造雷达干扰，干扰，阻塞与侵入
MILCAP	Military Capabilities	军事能力
MILMED	Military Medicine	军事医学
MIN	Minimum/Minute	最小/分
MIO	Maritime/Marine Interdiction Operation	海上封锁行动/拦截作战
MIOEX	Maritime/Marine Interdiction Operation Exercise	海上封锁行动/拦截作战演习
MISCEX	Miscellaneous Exercise	多科目混合演习
MIT	Maritime Inspection Training/Maritime Interception Training	海上检查训练/海上拦截训练
MIW	Mine Warfare	水雷战
MIWC	Mine Warfare Commander	水雷战指挥官
ML	Mile	里

续附表

缩略语/术语	英文全称	中文
MLA	Mean Line of Approach(Advance)/Mission Load Allowance	平均接近(前进)线/加载任务允许
MLC	Maritime Logistics Coordinator	海上后勤协调官
MLSE	Multinational Logistics Support Element	多国后勤支援分队
MLSO	Mutual Logistic Support Orders	后勤支援订单手册
MMAD	Marine Mammal Action Desk	海洋哺乳动物行动服务台
MMF	Minelayer, Fleet	舰队布雷舰
MMS	Mariner Squadron	陆战队分队
MMSI	Maritime Mobile Service Identity	海上移动通信业务标识
MMW	Millimeter Wave	毫米波
MNTF	Multinational Task Force	多国特混编队
MNV	Mine Neutralization Vehicle	灭雷器
MO	Medical Officer	军医
MOA	Memorandums of Agreement/Mutual Operations Area	协议备忘录/共同作战区
MOB	Man Over Board	人员落水
MOC	Maritime Operation Coordinator	海上行动协调官
MOD	Maximum Operating Depth/Modify/Moderate	最大作战深度/修改/适中, 四级风或浪
MODLOC	Modified Location	修改的位置
MOH	Material on Hand	手头资料
MOOTW	Military Operations Other Than War	非战争军事行动
MOTU	Mobile Technical Unit	机动技术单元
MOU	Memorandums of Understanding	理解备忘录
MOVREP	Movement Report	移动报告
MP	Military Police	宪兵
MPA	Maritime Patrol Aircraft	海上巡逻机
MPC	Materiel Processing Center/Middle Planning Conference	材料处理中心/中期计划会
MPEL	Multi-national Publications Electronic Library/Multi-national Publication List	多国出版物电子资料库/多国出版物列表
MPMBS	Method Passing Messages Between Ships	舰间通信方法
MPRA	Maritime Patrol and Reconnaissance Aircraft	海上巡逻与侦察机

续附表

缩略语/术语	英文全称	中文
MR	Medium Range	中距
MRCC	Maritime Rescue Coordination Centre	海上搜救协调中心
MRL	Maritime Rear Link	海上后方连接
MROC	Mobile Range Operations Center	机动范围作战中心
MRR	Manual Radio Relay/Minimum Risk Route	无线电中继指南/最小风险路径
MRS	Medium Range Sonar	中距声呐
MSALT	Military Support and Logistic Transport	军事支援与后勤运输
MSAT	Marine Species Awareness Training	海洋物种认知训练
MSC	Maritime Security Center	海上安全中心
MSD	Marine Sanitation Devices	海上卫生设备
MSE	Mobile Subscriber Equipment	机动订户装备
MSEL	Master Scenario Events List	演习想定项目
MSG	Marine Security Guard	海上安全警戒
MSG(S)	Message(s)	文电、信息
MSGID	Message Identification	信息识别
MSL	Missile/Mean Sea Level	导弹/平均海平面
MSN	Mission Number	任务编号
MSNDAT	Mission Data	任务数据
MSNLOC	Mission Location	任务位置
MSO	Maritime Security Operations/Minesweeper, Ocean	海上安全行动/远洋扫雷舰
MSOB	Maritime Special Operations Battalion	海上特种作战营
MSPF	Maritime Special Purpose Force	海上特种部队
MSS	Marine Sound Signals/Military Sealift Ship	海洋声响信号/军事海运舰船
MSST	Maritime Support Security Team	海上支援安全队
MSV	Multiple-Purpose Support Vessel	多用途辅助船
MT	Metric Ton	公吨
MTC	Mission Training Command	任务训练指挥
MTE	Major Training Exercise	主要训练演习
MTF	Medical Treatment Facility/Military Training Flight	医疗设备/检飞
MTI	Moving Target Indicator	移动目标指示器

续附表

缩略语/术语	英文全称	中文
MTOC	Maritime Tactical Operations Controller/Mobile Tactical Operations Center	海上战术行动指挥员/机动战术作战中心
MTOT	Mean Time on Target	瞄准平均时间
MUF	Maximum Usable Frequency	最大使用频率
MV	Motor Vessel	机动船
MW	Mine Warfare/Mega Watt	水雷战/兆瓦
MWC	Mine Warfare Coordinator	水雷战协调官
MWR	Missile Warning Receiver	导弹警告接收器
MZ	Military Zone	军事区
N	North	北
N/A	Not Available	不可用、未提供、无相关资料
NAS	National Air Space/Naval Air Station	国家领空/海军航空站
NASNI	Naval Air Station North Island (San Diego, California)	北岛海军航空站(加利福尼亚,圣迭戈)
NATO	North Atlantic Treaty Organization	北大西洋公约组织
NATOPS	Naval Air Training and Operating Procedures Standardization	海航训练和作战程序标准
NAV	Navigation/Navigator	航行/驾驶员
NAVAID	Navigation Aid	航行辅助
NAVAREA	Navigation Area	航行区域
NAVCALS	Naval Communications Area Local System	海军通信区域局域系统
NAVCAMC	Naval Computer and Message Center, Australia	澳大利亚海军计算机信息中心
NAVCAMS	Naval Communications Area Master Station	海军通信区主控站
NAVCOMPARS	Naval Communication Processing and Routing System	海军通信处理与规划系统
NAVCOMSTA	Naval Communications Station	海军通信站
NAVFAC	Naval Facilities	海军设施
NAVFOR	Naval Forces	海军部队
NAVHARS	Navigational Heading and Reference System	航行指向与参照系统
NAVINTSUMS	Naval Intelligence Summary	海军情报总结
NAVSSC	Naval Sea System Command	海军海上系统指挥部
NAVSECGRU	Naval Security Group	海军安全大队
NAVSTAR	Navigation Satellite Timing and Ranging	导航卫星计时与测距

续附表

缩略语/术语	英文全称	中文
NAVSUP	Naval Supply	海军补给
NBMC	Naval Base Medical Center	海军基地医疗中心
NCA	National Command Authority	国家指挥当局
NCAGS	Naval Cooperation and Guidance For Shipping	海军航运合作与指导
NCAPS	Naval Coordination and Protection of Shipping	海军航运协调与保护
NCDS	Naval Combat Data System	海军作战数据系统
NCHB	Naval Cargo Handling Battalion	海军货物递送营
NCMO	Non-Combat Military Operations	非作战军事行动
NCS	Naval Control of Shipping	海军航运控制
NCSORG	Naval Control of Shipping Organization	海军舰艇控制组织
NCTSI	Naval Center for Tactical Systems Interoperability, San Diego, California	加利福尼亚，圣迭戈，可互相操作战术系统海军中心
NDAA	National Defense Authorization Act	国防授权法案
NDMO	National Disaster Management Officer	国家救灾管理官
NDU	National Defense University	国防大学
NECC	Naval Expeditionary Combat Command	海军远征作战司令部
NEF	Naval Expeditionary Force	海上远征部队
NEO	Noncombat Evacuation Operation	非战斗撤离行动
NETC	Naval Education and Training Command	海军教育与训练司令部
NETF	Naval Expeditionary Task Force	海军远征军特混部队
NEX	Night Exercise	夜间演习
NFO	Naval Flight Officer	海军飞行员
NFWS	Navy Fighter Weapons School	海军战斗武器学校
NGA	National Geospatial-Intelligence Agency	[美]国家地理空间情报局
NGASN	Naval Gunfire Air Spotting Net	海军炮火离散网
NGFS/NGS	Naval Gun Fire Support/Naval Gunfire Support	海军炮火支援
NGLO	Naval Gunfire Liaison Officer	海军炮火联络官
NHC	Naval Health Clinic	海军健康中心
NIIP	Navy Instructional Input Program	海军指导输入计划
NIPO	Naval International Program Office	海军国际项目办公室
NIPRNET	Non-Classified Internet Protocol Router/Routing Network	公开网络协议路线网

续附表

缩略语/术语	英文全称	中文
NM	Nautical Mile	海里
NMAWC	Naval Mine and Anti-Submarine Warfare Command	海军水雷和反潜战司令部
NMC	Naval Medical Center/Naval Munitions Command/No Mission Capability	海军医疗中心/海军军需司令部/不具备任务能力
NO JOY	—	没有信息
NOAA	National Oceanic and Atmospheric Administration	国家海洋和大气管理局
NOACT	Navy Overseas Air Cargo Team	海军海外空运小组
NOPFWI	Naval Oceanographic Processing Facility Whidbey Island	威德比岛海军海洋处理站/场
NOSC	Navy On-Scene Coordinator	海军现场协调中心
NOTAL	Not to All	部分
NOTAM	Notice to Airmen	飞行员注意
NPC	Naval Police Center	海军宪兵中心
NPMOCEN	Naval Pacific Meteorological Center	海军太平洋气象中心
NPOC	Next Port of Call	下一港口
NRAD	Naval Research and Development	海军研究与发展
NRC	National Response Centre	国家应急中心
NROTC	Naval Reserve Officer Training Corps	海军后备军官训练团
NRRF	Naval Radio Receiving Facility	海军无线电接收设施
NRS	Naval Radio Station	海军无线电站
NSAW	Naval Strike and Air Warfare	海军打击和空战
NSFS	Naval Surface Fire Support	海军水面射击支援
NSM	Naval Strike Missile	海军打击导弹
NSO	Naval Special Operation/Normal Sustained Operation	海军特种作战/常规持续作战
NSTR	Nothing Significant to Report/Nothing Special to Report	无重要情况报告/无特殊情况报告
NSTS	National Secure Telephone System	国家安全电话系统
NSW	Naval Special Warfare	海洋特种作战
NSWC	Naval Surface Warfare Center	海军水面战中心
NSWG	Naval Special Warfare Group	海军特战大队
NSWU	Naval Special Warfare Unit	海军特战部队

续附表

缩略语/术语	英文全称	中文
NTCC	Naval Telecommunications Center	海军通信中心
NTCS-A	Naval Tactical Command System – Afloat	海军战术指挥系统-海上
NTDCP	Non-Tactical Data Collection Patch	非战术数据收集地
NTDS	Naval Tactical Data System	海军战术数据系统
NTISA	Navy Tactical Interoperability Support Activity	海军战术可相操作支援行动
NTTP	Navy Tactics, Techniques, and Procedures	海军战术，技术，程序
NTU	New Threat Upgrade	新威胁升级
NUPOC	Nuclear Propulsion Officer Candidate	核动力装置军官候补生
NVG	Night Vision Goggle	夜视仪
NW	Northwest	西北
NWDC	Navy Warfare Development Command	海军作战发展司令部
NWP	Naval Warfare Publication (United States Navy)	海军战术出版物
O/C	On Completion	完成后
O/O	On Order	按顺序
OB	Outboard	外舷
OBA	Oxygen Breathing Apparatus	呼吸装置
OBM	Out Board Motor	舷外引擎
OBS	Onboard Ship/Observation	登船/观察
OBSY	Observatory	气象台，天文台
OCA	Offensive Counter Air/Operational Control Authority	攻击性防空/作战控制授权
OCE	Officer Conducting the Exercise/Officer Controlling the Exercise	演习项目执行官/演习项目指挥官
OCM	Oil Content Monitors	油容量监视器
OCR	Optical Character Recognition	光学特征识别
OCS	Officer Conducting the Serial/Officer Candidate School	演习科目执行官/(海军)军官候补学校
ODT	Omni-Directional Transmission (Sonar)	全方位传递(声呐)
ODZ	Outer Defense Zone	外防御区
OFDA	Office of Foreign Disaster Assistance	国际救灾办公室
OFF STATION	—	离开阵位
OFF TASK	—	完成任务

续附表

缩略语/术语	英文全称	中文
OHS	Oil and Hazardous Substances	油料和危险物
OI	Operations Intelligence	(作战部门)情报分队
OIC	Officer in Charge	负责军官
OMFTS	Operational Maneuver from the Sea	海上作战机动
OMNI	Omni-Directional	全方位
ON STATION	—	就位
ONI	Office of Naval Intelligence	海军情报办公室
OOA	Out of Action/Out of Area	退出行动,丧失作战能力/出区
OOB	Order of Battle	战斗指令
OOD	Officer of the Deck	值更官
OOD(J)	Officer of the Deck(Junior)	值更官(副)
OPAREA(S)	Operating/Operational Area/Operations Areas	作战区
OPAS	Oil Pollution Abatement System	油污处理系统
OPCOM	Operational Command	作战指挥
OPCON	Operational Control	作战控制
OPDEC	Operational Deception	作战欺骗
OPDEF	Operational Defect	作战缺点
OPFOR	Opposing/Opposition Force	配合兵力/敌方部队
OPG	Operational Planning Group	作战计划小队
OPMGEN	Operational Message, General	通用作战信息
OPLAN	Operational Plan	作战计划
OP-N/OPS-NORMAL	Operation is Normal	行动正常
OPNAVINST	Operation Navy Instruction	海军作战指导
OPNOTE	Operations/Operational Note	作战备忘
OPO	Operations/Operations Officer	行动/作战军官
OPORD	Operations/Operational Order	作战命令
OPR	Office of Primary Responsibility	主要责任官
OPSEC	Operational Security	作战安全
OPSIG	Operating Signal	作战信号
OPSTAT	Operational Status	作战状态,作战地形

续附表

缩略语/术语	英文全称	中文
OPSUM	Operations/Operational Summary	综合日报
OPT	Operational Planning Team	行动计划小组
OPTCOMMS	Operation Task Commands	作战任务命令
ORM	Operational Risk Management	作战风险评估
OSC	On-Scene Commander/Operations Support Center	现场指挥官，现场协调官/作战支援中心
OSD	Office of the Under Secretary of Defense	[美]国防部副部长办公室
OSE	Officer Scheduling the Exercise/Officer of Serial Event	演习计划指挥官
OSG	Operational Support Group	作战支援大队
OSIS	Ocean Surveillance Information System	海洋监视信息系统
OSO	Operational Support Office	行动保障处
OTC	Officer in Tactical Control/Command	战术控制/战术指挥官
OTCIXS	Officer in Tactical Command Information Exchange System	战术指挥信息交换系统
OTH	Other/Over the Horizon	其他/超地平线
OTPI	On Top Position Indicator	高位指示器
OTSR	Optimum Track Ship Routing	最佳航线
OVBD	Overboard	落水
OWHT	Oily-Water Transfer System	含油废水转送系统
OWS	Oily Water Separators	油水分离器
PA	Patrol Area/Point Alpha/Public Affairs	巡逻海区/A点/公共事务
PACFLT	Pacific Fleet	[美海军]太平洋舰队
PACNORWEST	Pacific Northwest	西北太平洋
PACOM	Pacific Command	太平洋指挥部
PACV	Patrol Air Cushion Vessel	气垫巡逻艇
PAG	Pirate Action Group	海盗活动
PANCAKE	Pancake Landing	降落
PAO	Public Affairs Officer	公共事务官
PARA	Paragraph	段落
PAS	Passive Anti-Submarine Warfare System	被动反潜系统
PASC	Public Affairs Steering Committee	公共事务指挥委员会

续附表

缩略语/术语	英文全称	中文
PASSEP	Pass Separately	分开通过
PASSEX	Pass Exercise	通过训练
PAST	Private Armed Security	私人武装保安
PAX XFER	Personnel/Passager Transfer	人员输送
PB	Patrol Boat	巡逻艇
PC	Submarine Chaser	猎潜艇
PCMS	Passive Counter-Measures System	被动对抗系统
PCO	Prospective Commanding Officer	候任舰长
PCS	Position Course Speed	舰位、航向、航速
PD	Point Detonating	爆炸点
PDMS	Point-Defence Missile System	点防御导弹系统
PDX	Practice Depth Charge	深弹演练
PEARL HARBOR HI	Pearl Harbor Hickam	珍珠港希卡姆联合基地
PED	Personal Electronic Devices	携行电子设备
PFSO	Port Facility and Security Officer	港口设施保安员
PG	Patrol Gunboat	巡逻炮艇
PHIBRON	Amphibious Squadron	两栖中队
PHID	Positive Hostile Identification	主动对敌识别
PHM	Patrol Combatant-Missile, Hydrofoil	水翼导弹巡逻艇
PHOTOEX	Photo Exercise	航拍演习
PI	Personal Identifier	人员标识符
PIC	Potential Intelligence Collector	潜在情报收集者
PID	Positive Identification	主动识别
PIM	Position Intended Movement	预计航路
PIP	Predicted Intercept Point	预计拦截点
PIR	Priority Intelligence Requirements	预先情报需求
PIRAZ	Positive Identification Radar Advisory Zone	主动雷达识别区
PK	Probability of Kill	杀伤概率
PKO	Peace Keeping Operation	国际维和行动
PLA	People's Liberation Army	中国人民解放军
PLA(N)	People's Liberation Army (Navy)	中国人民解放军海军

续附表

缩略语/术语	英文全称	中文
PLB	Personnel Locator Beacon	人员定位标
PLT	Platoon	排
PMAP	Protective Measures Assessment Protocol	保护措施评估协议
PMRF	Pacific Missile Range Facility	太平洋导弹靶场
PN	Partner Nation	伙伴国家
PNCTR	Passive Non-Cooperative Target Recognition	被动非合作目标识别
POA	Pirate Operation Area	海盗活动区
POB	Personnel on Board/Pilot Onboard	舰上人员/引水员登舰
POC	Person of Contact/Point of Contact/Port of Call	联系人/联系点/访问港口
POD	Plan of the Day	一日工作计划
POE	Point of Entries	进入点
POL	Petroleum, Oils and Lubricants	油料
POSSUB	Possible Submarine	可能潜艇
POW	Prisoner of War	战争俘虏
PPI	Political Policy Indicators/Plan Position Indicator	官方政策风向标/平面位置显示器
PPLI	Positive Position, Location and Identification	主动定位和识别
PPR	Pre-Planned Responses	预置应对措施
PR	Personnel Recovery	人员救援
PRCC	Personnel Recovery Coordination Cell	人员救援协调单元
PRF	Pulse Repetition Frequency	脉冲重复频率
PRI	Primary	首要的
PRNOC	Pacific Region Network Operations Center	太平洋地区网络作战中心
PROBSUB	Probable Submarine	可能潜艇
PROP	Propeller	螺旋桨
PSI	Pounds per Square Inch	磅/平方英寸
PSK	Phase Shift Keying	相控转换键
PSN	Position	位置
PSO	Peace Support Operations	支援和平作战
PST	Port Side to	左舷靠
PSTN	Public Switched Telephone Network	公众交换电话网
PSYOPS	Psychological Operations	心理战

续附表

缩略语/术语	英文全称	中文
Pt	Point	点,句号
PU	Participating Unit(on Data Link)	参与节点(数据链)
PVST	Port Visit	访问港口
PVTC	Private Chat	私聊
PWC	Pacific Warfare Center	太平洋作战中心
PXO	Prospective Executive Officer	即将就任的副舰长
QM	Quartermaster	军需官,操舵兵
QMOW	Quartermaster on Watch	当更车钟手
QNH	Barometric Pressure Adjusted to Sea Level	修正海平面气压
QR	Quick Reaction	快速反应
QRC	Quick Release Coupling	速开连接装置
QTR	Quarter	尾部
QTY	Quantity	数量
QUAL	Quality	质量,资格
R/T	Radiotelephone	无线电话
R/V	Receiving Vessel	补给接收船
R2	Rapid Response and Reporting	快速反应与报告
RADALT	Radio Altimeter	无线电高度计
RADC	Regional Air Defence Commander	区域防空指挥官
RADHAZ	Radio (Frequency) Hazard	无线电(频率)冒险
RADSTA	Radio Station	无线电站
RAF	Royal Air Force	皇家空军
RAIDEX	Air Defense Exercise for Air vs Surface Raids	空中和水面突出下的防空演习
RAM	Rolling Airframe Missile	滚动弹体导弹
RAN	Royal Australian Navy	澳大利亚皇家海军
RAP	Recognized Control Picture	经过验证的控制图
RAS	Replenishment at Sea	海上补给
RAS-A	Replenishment at Sea Ammunition	补给弹药
RAS-F	Replenishment at Sea Fuel	补给燃油
RAS-S	Replenishment at Sea Stores	补给备品
RAS-T	Replenishment at Sea Fleet Freight	补给货物

续附表

缩略语/术语	英文全称	中文
RAS-V	Replenishment at Sea Fresh Fruit and Vegetables	补给新鲜水果和蔬菜
RASREQ	Replenishment at Sea Requirement	航行补给需求
RDC	Recruit Division Commander	分队指挥
RDS	Rounds	弹药数
RDT	Rotating Directional Transmission	旋转发射器
RECON	Reconnaissance	侦察
REF	References	参考
REL	Releasable	可发射
REPINST	Reporting Instructions	报告指导
REPOS	Reposition	位置调整
RESCAP	Rescue Combat Air Patrol	救援战空中巡逻
RESCORT	Rescue Escort	救援护航
RESDES	Rescue Destroyer	救援驱逐舰
RF	Radio Frequency	无线电频率
RFA	Restricted Fire Area	限制射击区
RG	Range	范围,量程
RGR	Roger	收到
RHAWS	Radar Homing and Warning System	雷达自动导引与告警系统
RHIB	Ragid Hull Inflatable Boat	硬壳充气艇(橡皮艇)
RIMPAC	Rim of the Pacific	环太平洋
RJTAGS	Remote Joint Theater Air Ground System	联合战区远程空地系统
RM	Radioman	无线电操作员
RMKS	Remarks	备注
RMP	Recognized Maritime Picture/Regional Monitoring Program	识别海上照片/区域监控
RN	Royal Navy	皇家海军
RNCS	Regional Naval Control of Shipping	区域海军航运控制
RNDV	Rendezvous	会合点
RNZN	Royal New Zealand Navy	新西兰皇家海军
ROA	Radius of Action	行动半径
ROCC	Range Operations Control Center	远程作战控制中心
RODEO(NSFS)	Rodeo=Cowboy(Naval Ship Fire Support)	主炮射击比赛

续附表

缩略语/术语	英文全称	中文
ROE	Rules of Engagement	交战规则
ROKN	Republic of Korean Navy	韩国海军
RO-RO	Roll-on Roll-off	滚装船
ROV	Remotely Operated Vehicle	遥控机器人
RP	Republic of the Philippines/Rocket Projectile	菲律宾/抛射火箭
RPM	Revolutions per Minute	每分钟转速
RPV	Remotely Piloted Vehicle	遥控飞行器
RQ	Reception Quality	接收质量
RRC	Regional Reporting Center	区域报告中心
RRR	Rapid Runway Repair	快速跑道修复
RRR(R)	Rotors Running Refuelling (and Rearining)	旋翼不停情况下加油和挂弹
RSC	Radar System Controller	雷达系统控制器
RSI	Radiation Status Indicator	辐射状态指示器
RSO&I	Reception, Staging, Onward Movement and Integration	接收、展现、前进移动与集成
RSS	Republic of Singapore Ship	新加坡军舰
RTDC	Rocket Thrown Depth Charge	火箭深弹
RTF	Return to Force	返回部队
RTN	Royal Thailand Naval Ship	泰国皇家海军舰艇
RTP	Return to Port	返港/靠港
RTT	Rocket Thrown Torpedo	火箭助推鱼雷
RVA	Request Visit Authorization	访问需求授权中心
RW	Rotary Wing	旋转翼
RWR	Radar Warning Receiver	雷达告警接收机
S	South	南
S.S.	Steamship	汽船，轮船
S/S	Ship/Store	舰/备品
SA	Situational Awareness/Strike Attack (Aircraft)/Surveillance Area	态势告警/空中攻击/监视区
SAA	Submarine Action Area	潜艇行动区
SAAR	System Authorization Access Request	系统授权接入请求

续附表

缩略语/术语	英文全称	中文
SAC	Scene of Action Commander/Shipborne Air Controller/Special Alert Criteria	现场行动指挥/舰载空中指挥官/专用告警边界
SACC	Supporting Arms Coordination Center	支援武器协调中心
SADC	Sector Air Defense Commander	区域防空指挥官
SAFE	Selected Areas for Evasion	既定撤退区
SAG	Surface Attack Group/Surface Action Group	水面攻击大队/水面行动大队
SAGC	Surface Action Group Commander	水面作战群司令
SAM	Surface to Air Missile	舰对空导弹
SAMEX	Surface to Air Missile Exercise	舰空导弹演习
SAR	Search and Rescue	搜救
SARDO	Search and Rescue Duty Officer	搜救值更官
SARIR	Search and Rescue Incident Report	搜救事件报告
SARREQ	Search and Rescue Request	搜救请求
SARSIT	Search and Rescue Situation Summary	搜救状态总结
SARTF	Search and Rescue Task Force	搜救特混编队
SARTIS	Ships Advanced Radar Target Identification System	舰载雷达目标识别系统
SAS	Safety Approach Sector/Special Air Service	安全接近区/特别空勤队
SAT	Satellite/Submarine Advisory Team	卫星/潜艇咨询小组
SAT/UNSAT	Satisfaction/Unsatisfaction=Good/No good	满意/不满意
SATCOM	Satellite Communication	卫星通信
SATNAV	Satellite Navigation	卫星导航
SATVUL	Satellite Vulnerability	卫星弱点
SAU	Surface Action Unit	水面行动兵力
SAUC	Search Attack Unit Commander	搜寻攻击小队司令
SAWC	Surface Air Warfare Commander	水面防空指挥官
SAWWS	Sewage and Waste Water System	污水与废水处理系统
SB	Safety Berth	安全泊位
SBMSS	Shore Based Message Service System	岸基信息服务系统
SC	Search and Rescue Coordinator/Screen Commander	搜救协调官/警戒部队指挥官
SCA	Space Coordination Authority	空间协调授权

续附表

缩略语/术语	英文全称	中文
SCC	Sea Combat Commander/Surface Capability Check/Surface Combat Condition	海上战斗指挥官/(直升机)检飞/水面舰艇作战状态
SCF	Surface Combatant Force	海上作战部队
SCI	Sensitive Compartmentalized Information	灵敏区分信息
SCRN	Screen	警戒
SDC	Sonar Data Computer	声呐数据计算机
SE	Southeast	东南
SEAD	Suppression of Enemy Air Defenses	对敌方防空火力的压制
SEAL	Sea-Air-Land Team	"海豹"分队
SEALOGC	Sea Logistic Command	海上后勤司令部
SEC	Submarine Element Coordinator	潜艇单元协调官
SEC DET	Security Detachment	安全分队
SECDEF	Secretary of Defense	[美]国防部长
SENSO	Sensor Operator	传感器操作员
SEP	Sea Exercise Program	海上演习计划
SEPCOR	Separate Coordinate	独立坐标点
SEPTAR	Surface Engagement Practice Target	太平洋目标水面交战
SERC	The State of Hawaii Emergency Response Commission	夏威夷州应急反应委员会
SFCS	Submarine Fire Control System	潜艇火控系统
SGSA	Submarine Generated Search Area	潜艇探索区
SHAR	Sea Harrier	海鹞式飞机
SHF	Super High Frequency	超高频
SHML	Ship's Hazardous Material List	船舶危险品清单
SI	Sailing Instruction/Special Intelligence	航行细则/专用情报
SIC	Subject Identification Code	科目识别码
SID(S)	Subscriber Identification (System)	用户识别(系统)
SIF	Selective Identification Feature	选择识别特征
SIGINT	Signal Intelligence	通信情报,信号情报
SIGSEC	Signal Security	信号安全
SIM	Submarine Intended Movement	潜艇运动意图
SINKEX	Sinking Exercise	舰艇击沉演习

续附表

缩略语/术语	英文全称	中文
SIO	Shipboard Intelligence Officer	舰载情报官
SIPRNET	Secret Internet Protocol Routing/Router Network	秘密网络协议路线网络
SIT	Situation	形势
SITREP	Situation Reports	情况报告
SL	Safe Line	安全航线
SLAM	Standoff Land Attack Missile	平衡对陆攻击导弹
SLOC	Sea Lines of Communication	海上交通线
SLT	Ship Launched Torpedo	舰射鱼雷
SLW	Slow	缓慢
SM	Standard Missile	标准导弹
SMAW	Shoulder Mounted Assault Weapon	肩扛攻击武器
SMC	Search and Rescue Mission Coordinator	搜救任务协调官
SMCM	Surface Mine Countermeasures	水面舰艇水雷战
SMCP	Standard Marine Communication Phrases	标准海上通信用语
SME	Significant Military Equipment	重大军事装备
SNODUF	Signal not to be Used for Direction Finding	非方向指向信号
SOA	Speed of Advance	前进速度
SOC	Special Operations Capablity	有特种作战能力的
SOCCE	Special Operations Command and Control Element	特种作战指挥与控制小队
SOE	Sequence/Schedule of Events/Serial of Events	演习计划/项目计划
SOF	Special Operations Forces	特种作战部队，特种兵
SOFLE	Special Operations Foreign Land Element	特种作战外国地面部队
SOIS	Special Operations Instructions	特种作战指导
SOLE	Special Operations Land Element	特种作战地面部队
SOM	Scheme of Maneuver	机动计划
SOMF	Start of Message Functions	消息开始作用
SOP	Standard Operating Procedure	标准操作程序
SOPA	Senior Officer Present Afloat/Ashore	海上/港岸现场最高军官
SOTA	Sigint（Signal Intelligence）Operational Tasking Authority	信号情报作战任务授权
SOTF	Special Operations Task Force	特种作战特混部队

续附表

缩略语/术语	英文全称	中文
SP	Suspected Pirate/Speed	海盗嫌疑人/速度
SPA	Submarine Patrol Area/Submarine Probability Area	潜艇巡逻区/潜艇可能区
SPECINST	Special Instruction	专项指导
SROE	Standing Rules of Engagement	固定交战规则
SRU	Search and Rescue Unit	搜救单元
SRV	Severe Risk Vessel	高危商船
SSAS	Ship Security Alert System	船舶安保警报系统
SSBN	Strategic Submarine Ballistic Nuclear	弹道导弹战略核潜艇
SSC	Sea Surveillance and Control/Special Security Center	海上监视与控制/特别安全中心
SSDE	Diesel-Electric Submarines	柴电潜艇
SSES	Ship's Signal Exploitation Space	舰载信号开发空间
SSIXS	Submarine Satellite Information Exchange System	潜艇卫星情报交换系统
SSLOI	Submarine Safety Letter of Instruction	潜艇安全指导书
SSM	Surface to Surface Missile	舰舰导弹
SSN	Submarine Nuclear	攻击型核潜艇
SSN(DS)	Submarine Nuclear in Direct Support	直接支援攻击型核潜艇
SSO	Ship Security Officer	船舶安保员
SSP	Ship's Security Plan	船舶安保计划
SSR	Safety Surveillance and Reporting	安全监视报告
SSSC	Surface & Subsurface Surveillance and Coordination	水面与水下监视与协调
SST	Starboard Side to	右舷靠
SSUS	Sound Surveillance Underwater System	水下音响监测系统
ST	Support Transit	支援通过
STAFFEX	Staff Exercise	参谋演习
STAO	Staff Tactical Action Officer	参谋战术行动官
STO	Systems Test Officer	系统检测官
STOVL	Short Takeoff	短距离起飞
STT	Shore Targeting Terminal	海滨瞄准终端
STUFT	Ships Taken Up from Trade	贸易征召船
STWS	Ship Torpedo Weapon System	舰载鱼雷武器系统

续附表

缩略语/术语	英文全称	中文
SU	Surface	水面
SUA	Special Use Airspace	专用空域
SUBJ	Subject	目标，下发
SUBOPAUTH	Submarine Operating Authority	潜艇操作指挥部
SUBROC	Submarine Rocket	"萨布洛克"反潜火箭
SUBRV	Substantial Risk Vessel	较危商船
SUPSIT	Support Situation	支援情况
SURFEX	Surface Exercise	水面演习
SURG	Surgeon	军医，外科医生
SURTASS	Surface Towed Array System	水面舰艇拖曳阵列系统
SUS	Signal Underwater Sound	水下声响信号
SUSTEX	Sustainment Exercise	持续演练
SUW	Surface Warfare	水面作战
SUWC	Surface Warfare Commander	水面作战指挥官
SUWEX	Surface Warfare Exercise	水面作战演习
SVC	Service	服役
SVT	Surface Vessel Target	水面船只目标
SVTT	Surface Vessel Torpedo Tube	水面舰艇鱼雷管
SW	Shallow Water/Short Wave/Surface Warfare	浅水/短波/水面作战
SWARMEX	Numerous Small Boats Attacking As a Swarm	集群小船攻击
SWC	Ship's Weapons Coordinator	舰载武器协调官
SWWCAAS	Ships Wastewater Collection Ashore Abatement System	舰艇废水收集、海滨减轻污染系统
SYNTEX	Synthesis/Synthetic Exercise	通信（综合）/情报演习
T/O	Table of Organization/Take Over	组织结构/交接（重在接）
TACDI	Tactical Direction for Maritime Strike/Attack	海上打击/攻击战术指导
TASW	Theater Anti-Submarine Warfare	战区反潜战
TBA	To be Announced	待宣布
TBC	To be Checked	待核对
TBD	To be Determined	待定
TEMP	Temperature	温度
TEMPO	Temporary	临时的
TET	Targeting Effects Team	目标效果小组

续附表

缩略语/术语	英文全称	中文
TG	Task Group	特混大队
TGT	Target	目标
TOC	Tactical Operations Controller	战术行动指挥官
TOFF	Take Off	起飞
TORPEX	Torpedo Exercise	鱼雷演习
TOT	Time On/Over Target	抵达目标时间
TRP	Troop Lift	兵力输送
TSS	Traffic Seperation Scheme	分道通航制
TST	Transit	航渡
TTA	Tactical Training Assessment	战术训练评估
TTGP	Tactical Training Group Pacific	太平洋战术训练小组
TTP	Tactics, Techniques and Procedures	战术、技术和规程
TTW	Territorial Waters	领海
TTX	Table Top Exercise	图上推演
TU	Task Unit	特混小队
TUSWC	Theatre Undersea Warfare Commander	战区反潜战指挥官
TW	True Wind	真风向
TWC	Threat Warning Condition	威胁报警条件
TWO	Tactical Watch Officer	战斗值班军官
TY	Thank You	谢谢
U/W	Underway	航渡
UAV	Unmanned Aerial Vehicle	无人机
UMCMC	Unmanned Mine Countermeasure Command	无人反水雷司令部
UN HCR	United Nations High Commissioner for Refugees	联合国难民高级理事
UN OCHA	United Nations Office for Coordination of Humanitarian Assistance	联合国人道主义援助协调办公室
UNCLAS	Unclassified	非保密、公开
UNCLOS	United Nations Convention on the Law of the Sea 1982	1982年《联合国海洋法公约》
UNKN	Unknown	未知
UN-OCHA	United Nations Office for the Coordination of Humanitarian Affairs	联合国人道主义事务协调处
UNODIR	Unless Otherwise Directed	除非另外引导
UNREP	Underway Replenishment	航行补给
UNSC	United Nations Security Council	联合国安全理事会
UPU	Universal Postal Union	万国邮政联盟

续附表

缩略语/术语	英文全称	中文
URG	Underway Replenishment Group	航行补给小组
USCG	United States Coast Guard	美国海岸警卫队
USE	Uncommon Stranding Event	非正常搁浅事件
USMC	United States Marine Corps	美国海军陆战队
USMTF	United States Message Text Formatting	美军文本信息格式
USNAVCENT	United States Naval Forces Central Command	美国海军部队中央司令部
USNS	United States Naval Service	美国海军勤务
USS	United States Ship	美国舰艇
USTC	United States Transportation Command	美国运输司令部
USWEX	Undersea Warfare Exercise	反潜战演习
UTC	Universal Time Coordinated	世界时
UUV	Unmanned Underwater Vehicle	无人操纵潜水器
UW	Unconventional Warfare/Underway (From Pier/Anchorage)	非常规作战/航渡(从码头/锚地)
UW-FP	Underway, Conducting Force Protection Exercise	航渡兵力保护演习
UXO	Unexploded Ordnance	未爆炸弹
V/CCTF	Vice Commander Combined Task Force	联合特混部队副司令
V/S	Visual Signaling	视觉信号
VA	Attack Aircraft Squadron/Vital Area	战斗机攻击中队/关键区域
VAQ	Electronic Warfare Squadron	电子战中队
VAR	Visitor Authorization Request	参观授权申请
VBSS	Verification, Boarding, Search and Seizure	临检拿捕
VBSS(H/S)(TT)	Verification, Boarding, Search and Seizure (Helicopter/Surface) (Training Team)	登临检查小组(直升机/小艇)(训练小组)
VECTAC	Vectored Attack (Anti-Surface Warfare)	无线电导航攻击(反水面战)
VERTREP	Vertical Replenishment	垂直补给
VFR	Visual Flight Rules	目力航行规则
VHF	Very High Frequency	甚高频
VIB	Verify in Ballast	校正弹道
VINSON	Very High Frequency Secure Voice System	甚高频安全语音系统
VIRIN	Visual Record Identification Number	目力记录识别码
VIS	Visibility	能见度

续附表

缩略语/术语	英文全称	中文
VL	Vertical Landing	垂直降落
VLF	Very Low Frequency	甚低频
VLS	Vertical Launch System	垂直发射系统
VMA	Marine Attack Squadron	海上打击中队
VMC	Visual Meteorological Condition	视觉估算的气象条件
VOCODER	Voice Coder	语音编码器
VOI	Vessel of Interest	嫌疑船员
VOIP	Voice Over Internet Protocol	语音通信网络协定
VOR	Very High Frequency Omni-Directional Range	甚高频全方位覆盖
VP	Fixed Wing Patrol	固定翼巡逻机
VPD	Vessel Protection Detachment	随船护卫分队
VQ	Electronic Warfare Squadron/Fixed Wing Reconnaissance/Reconnaissance Aircraft Squadron	电子战中队/固定翼侦察机/侦察机中队
VSL	Vessel/Vulnerable Ship List	舰船/易受攻击的船舶名单
VSW	Very Shallow Water	很浅的水域
VTS	Vessel Traffic System	船舶交通服务台
VULPER	Vulnerability Period	易受攻击阶段
W	west/with	西/和，伴随
WASEX	War at Sea Exercise/Wide Area Surveillance Exercise	海战演习/广域监视演习
WC	Warfare Commander	作战指挥员
WEAX	Weather Forecast	天气预报
WEZ	Weapon Engagement Zone	武器使用区
WFO	Without Further Orders	没有进一步命令
WILCO	Will Comply(＝Roger)	照办
WL	Waterline	水线
WLY	Westerly	偏西
WMD	Weapon of Mass Destruction	大规模杀伤性武器
WMO	World Meteorological Organization	世界气象组织
WOG Day	the Cross Line Day	舰员第一次穿越赤道的纪念活动日
WPN	Weapon	武器

续附表

缩略语/术语	英文全称	中文
WPNS	Western Pacific Naval Symposium	西太平洋海岛论坛
WRNG	Warning	警告，警报
WRR	Weapons Release Range	武器发射范围
WSO	Warfighter Support Office	作战人员保障办公室
WSW	West-South-West	西南西
WWMCS	World Wide Military Communication System	全球军事信息系统
WX	Weather(Information)	天气
XFER	Transfer	传递
XMIT	Transmit	传播
XO	Executive Officer	副指挥官，副舰长
XSIT	Transit	航渡
XTF	Executive to Follow	准备执行
YDS	Yards	码
Z/GMT	Greenwich Mean Time	世界时，格林威治平时

参考文献

陈安刚，金之刚. 中法海军首次联演扫描[J]. 舰载武器，2004(4)：16-17.

陈安刚. 透视中印海军首次联合演习[J]. 现代舰船，2004(1)：4-5.

杜农一，周辉，杨凯. 新中国军事外交与国际维和研究[M]. 北京：国防大学出版社，2015.

樊高月. 美军联合作战与联合训练[M]. 北京：解放军出版社，2000.

冯金波，吴铁民，张波. 军事演习巡礼：体验军力提升的重要环节[M]. 郑州：文心出版社，2016.

韩旭东. 日印联演的战略考量[N]. 解放军报，2012-05-06(004).

黄伟文. 联合作战指挥[M]. 北京：海潮出版社，2010.

贾英新. 军事演习炸点系统的设计与实现[D]. 北京：北京工业大学，2012.

金日. 多国海上联合军演的组织与实施[J]. 舰船知识，2013(9)：30-32.

金正昆. 外交学[M]. 北京：中国人民大学出版社，2004.

孔令丰，范嘉宾. 计算机模拟战役对抗演习概论[M]. 北京：国防大学出版社，2001.

李大光. 联演的新趋势[J]. 时事报告，2014(8)：54-55.

李大光. 走近还是远离战争——21世纪中国周边军事演习点评[M]. 武汉：长江文艺出版社，2017.

李大鹏. "海上联合-2015"中俄联演实现了哪些新突破[N]. 中国青年报，2015-10-09(009).

李繁杰. 中美海上矛盾与合作前景[J]. 国际问题研究，2013(11)：79-89.

李辉光. 外国军事演习概览[M]. 北京：军事科学院出版社，2004.

李庆山，李辉光. 122个国家军事演习内幕[M]. 北京：中共党史出版社，2008.

刘永，文广. 美军联演四问[J]. 环球军事，2010(8)：15-17.

罗铮. 融合度更深 实战味更浓 新装备更多[N]. 解放军报，2014-05-20(003).

史滇生. 世界海军军事史概论[M]. 北京：海潮出版社，2003.

孙涛，王岩，金慧玉，等. "和平方舟"号医院船参加"环太平洋-2016"联演实践与思考[J]. 军事医学，2016(11)：857-859.

万发扬. 中国军事外交理论与实践[M]. 北京：时事出版社，2014.

王迪. 中外联合演习新闻报道研究文献综述[J]. 新闻世界, 2015(10): 125-126.

吴义福, 李宇宙, 钟魁润. 中美海军首次举行海上通信联演[J]. 当代海军, 2006(11): 4-7.

吴振. 战争设计工程方法在军事演习方案设计中的应用研究[D]. 长沙: 国防科学技术大学, 2009.

杨涛, 邱亚宁. 新中国60年中外联演的实践与启示[C]//中共中央文献研究室科研管理部. 新中国60年研究文集(2). 北京: 中共中央文献研究室科研管理部, 2009.

尹庆文, 曹晓霞. 如何提高演习报道的时效性[J]. 军事记者, 2008(6): 34-35.

游海. 实兵演习安全风险专家预评估系统设计与实现[D]. 郑州: 郑州大学, 2011.

张启良. 海军外交论[M]. 北京: 军事科学出版社, 2013.

张强. 仅靠计算机模拟能达成演习目的吗?[N]. 科技日报, 2016-06-07(003).

张玥, 王建华, 李宇庆. "和平友谊-2015"联演的三重意义[N]. 中国青年报, 2015-09-25(009).

周从保, 钟海. 军事外交战略研究[M]. 北京: 国防大学出版社, 2015.

周月星. 在破解难题中提高海防管控联演联训质量[J]. 国防, 2016(5): 72-74.

后 记

夕阳西坠,余晖点点,海面波光粼粼。远处,天水之间留下一条丝带般的红,似被火焰舔舐过的刀锋,在海面淬火。遥想当年,在随返航的战舰乘风破浪奔赴祖国母亲怀抱的征程中,我与梁阳兄长每每散步于直升机甲板之上,探讨着环太平洋联演中的"趣事"。太平洋上咸咸的海风拂过,深入浅出的交谈,使我陷入思考……

与世界强国海军同行同台竞技、交流合作,让我强烈感受到国家兴盛对实现强军梦、海军梦的强烈召唤,感受到成长壮大的中国海军在挺进深蓝道路上所面临的机遇挑战,感受到建设世界一流海军的历史使命重任在肩。新时代的人民海军,早已劈波犁浪,挺进大洋,履行大国担当,不仅吸引世人的注目,也成为国人眼中的焦点。自己内心酝酿已久的想法也怦然迸发,想做一些实事,让更多的民众,特别是热血青年多维地了解海军,关注海上联演,投身壮美的海军事业,培养和储备海上联演人才。

组织和参加海上联演是海军建设的重要课题,《海上联演常识100问》整理解答了海上联演解码、筹划、实施、展望四个方面100个常见问题,并附录了国外重大海上联演概览、海上联演常用英语300句、缩略语等素材,意在科普宣传,为青年军事"发烧友"和希望知晓海上联演基础知识的朋友提供"解渴之梅",为广大读者了解海军及海上联演对构建海洋命运共同体的重要性贡献微薄力量。

本书编写工作离不开各级领导和同事的大力支持。原海军新闻发言人梁阳欣然为本书作序,海军工程大学尹敬湘副教授协助完成书稿纲目拟定和全书统稿、审稿,姜俊、程飞霞、段恪忞在前期研究工作中做了大量基础性工作,吴彦彬、聂忠参与了许多重要内容的修订,金倩、马岚、孔德霖、郭鹏收集汇总了有关附件,龚梅副译审对英语内容进行了订正。在这里,还要给海军工程大学优秀的特色素质创新俱乐部——"深蓝国际工场"历届骨干及大学首批赴外地参观来访军舰的"青新分队"全体成员点赞,他们与本书主创人员积极探讨，就"100问"题库的建设与完善进行头脑风暴，并主动思考、协助完成部分题目答案。海洋出版社对本书出版给予了宝贵支持。在此，谨对所有给予本书帮助支持的单位和个人表示衷心的感谢。

  由于时间仓促、水平有限，难免挂一漏万，如有错漏和不当之处，敬请读者朋友批评指正。

编者于武汉